Tales *from the* Hump

A Kid's-eye View of the 60s

a memoir

Richard J. Morgan

Tales from the Hump
Copyright © 2024 by Richard J. Morgan.

All rights reserved. No part of this publication may be reproduced, distributed or transmitted in any form or by any means, including photocopying, recording, or other electronic or mechanical methods, without the prior written permission of the publisher, except in the case of brief quotations embodied in critical reviews and certain other noncommercial uses permitted by copyright law.

ISBN: 979-8-9915898-1-9 (paperback)
ISBN: 979-8-9915898-0-2 (ebook)

Book Cover Design and Interior Formatting by 100Covers.

*To my wife Jeanne, who said
"Why don't you write this stuff down?"*

Acknowledgements

I'd like to thank my wife Jeanne for her encouragement and nonstop support. Also to my beta readers: Dyrk Ashton, Jeri Kessenich, and Richard Kallenbach, who gave me such valuable feedback. Also a big thank you to the Port Clinton Writers' Circle for their ongoing encouragement and help. I could have not written this without them. And for all the people in my life who contributed to all the events described in this book.

Contents

Dedication iii
Acknowledgements v
Why Tales from the Hump? 1
A Little Biography 5
Age 5 and 6 7
    The Times That Built Me 8
    I'm Never Going to Grow Up 10
    Alien 13
    Mom, Where Were You? 16
    JoJo 18
    Andy. And Dandy. 22
    My Toy Guns 26
    Family Photo 30
    Mom's Wisdom, Part 1 32
    Telling Time. 35
    All Adult Men Are Named Warren 39
    How Did She Know? 40
    Cookie 43
    See You Next Year 47
    The Birds and the Bees 49
    A Whole Penny 52
    Piano Lessons. 55
California 59
    We're Going to Disneyland. 60
    This Land Is Your Land. 63

 Colorado Springs 65
 Random Stops. 68
 A Trip to the Moon 71
Age 7 and 8 73
 Rusty 74
 Mail 78
 Gravity 80
 The Chocolate Bunny 82
 Milky Way 86
 July 20, 1963 88
 JFK 91
 My Early Bikes 93
 The Cottage 97
 Soaky 101
 Swimming Lessons 104
 Second Grade 108
 A Very Bad Day (But It Could Have Been Worse) . . . 112
 How Fast Is 5 MPH? 115
 Kenny's Market 119
 My Paper Route, Part 1 122
 My Paper Route, Part 2 127
 My Paper Route, Part 3 130
 Grandpa Jack and Grandma Dutch 133
 Herman 136
 Carp Hunting 142
 My Piano Teacher's Cat 145
 Cocoa 147
 Pears… and More 150
Age 9 and 10 155
 Mom's Wisdom, Part 2 156
 Sohio 159

Tent Sales. 161
Fishing 165
Music Class. 168
Why Are There Commercials?. 171
Sidewalk Sales 173
Good Friday Easter Eggs. 176
Easter Morning Easter Eggs 179
The Pinewood Derby. 183
A Partridge in a Pear Tree. 187
Camp Miakonda 190
Of Batteries and Bulbs 194
I Got You Last 197
Fifth Grade School Birthday Party 199
The Jump That Wasn't 201
The Rifle Matches 206
The Charcoal Grill 209
Rockets. 210

Age 11 215
My Best Bike 216
Sixth Grade 219
Last Day for Lunch 223

Age 12 and 13: Junior High 227
The First Day of Phys Ed. 228
I Learned a Lesson 232
The Worst Christmas Program 235
Girls. 238
Roller Skating. 243
A Trip to Remember 246

Afterword. 251

Why Tales from the Hump?

Morgan family home, with Cathy and Pat, 1953

I grew up in the 60s, when the world was…not what it is today. Better or worse is for you to decide, but it definitely was different.

In the 60s, nobody had a van. Unless you owned a repair business or something. My dad, for instance, had a small business called Morgan's TV. So he had a work van, complete with his logo, phone number, and *"Follow me to Morgan's TV* painted on it.

I didn't know one family who had a van as a family vehicle. I'm not sure that was even a thing. There were no SUVs. Nope, every family I knew had one of two cars: a four-door sedan or a station wagon.

When I was real little, I'm sure we had a sedan. Just one. Yes, there were four kids—but only one car, because Mom didn't have a driver's license. At least not at first. She got one eventually, of course. While it's hard to imagine now, it was fairly common for the mom of the house to not drive. Don't ask me how they got all their errands done. I have no idea. (Although I'm convinced that moms in the 50s and 60s were pretty much all super women.) Mom eventually did have a car. It was a red Mercury station wagon. But the family car as I remember it was a Buick LeSabre. It was a big car. Which was good, because with four kids, we needed lots of room.

Okay, where do all these people sit? Good question. For starters, Dad drove. Always. Even after Mom got her license, Dad drove. (After all, wasn't driving a man's job?) So Dad had the driver's seat. Mom was in the passenger seat. How about the rest of us? Well, the oldest kid, my sister Pat, always sat in the back by the passenger-side window. Cathy, the next oldest, got the driver's-side seat in the back. Jeff, next in line, sat in front. Yes, the front. Back then, bucket seats were not a thing, at least not for family cars. So Jeff sat in the front between Mom and Dad. Sometimes he even switched with Mom. Why was Jeff in the front? Because he *said* he got carsick if he sat in the back. I never really believed it. I figured he just said that so he didn't have to sit in the back seat. Even today, sixty years later, he still never sits in the back seat. Ever. So maybe he was telling the truth. I guess maybe I can believe him now.

Where did that leave me? You guessed it: in the back, in the middle. I was the "baby," so I got the worst seat. And it was no fun. Cars didn't have air conditioning back then, *and* both my parents smoked. If you didn't live through those times, you probably have no idea how prevalent smoking was in the 60s. Almost every adult smoked. And they smoked just about everywhere—restaurants, the house, cars, libraries, laundromats—everywhere. Even around kids. Secondhand smoke was not a concept back then. So whenever we went anywhere, I was stuck in the middle in the back, with no fresh air. And no view.

But the worst part was "the hump." Most cars are front-wheel-drive now. That wasn't the case in the 60s. So there had to be a way to get the power from the engine, which was in the front, to the rear wheels. The drive shaft ran the length of the car, which caused a hump in the middle. Most modern cars still have that feature, but it's *much* smaller than it was then. So when I rode in the middle of the back, I rode on the hump. Now, I was little, so I didn't need much leg room. But I needed some. And I really didn't have it. While my sisters and brother got to open the windows for fresh air, and to look out, I had none of that.

I saw the world from the hump.

Did I ever complain? Of course I did. Quite often. But here's how this argument went, pretty much every time:

Me: I'm tired of sitting in the middle. Cathy, can you trade with me?
Cathy: No.
Me: Come on. Please? I'm tired of sitting here.
Cathy: Nope.
Me: *Please?* Mom, Cathy won't let me—
Dad (yelling): You kids shut up and quit arguing. I'm tired of hearing it. Do you want a spanking?
Cathy: (Smiles an evil smile at me)

I never won. And the girls never lost. Wonderful.

As a side note, I relayed this thought to my dad many years later, and to be fair, he felt bad. He said I should've come to him and explained. Well, I never thought of that (I was a kid.) And I'm not sure it would have done any good. Maybe.

Regardless, I saw the world from the hump.

This book started as my memories of things that happened while our family was driving. However, a lot of things weren't related to the car. So I added other stories. All these actually happened, at least to the best of my memory. And I can remember a lot. My sister Pat, who's about six years older than me, said she can't remember much about these instances at all. Which doesn't make sense really, since you'd think a twelve-year-old would remember more about a particular happening than a six-year-old. Her therapist told her that maybe I had a happier childhood, so these memories mean more to me. Maybe.

I must have had a great childhood! I guess you can be the judge.

A Little Biography

The Morgan Family, left to right: Cathy, Jeff, Pat, Thecla, Dick, Warren

When I was little, as now, I lived in northwest Ohio, in Port Clinton, a small town on Lake Erie. It's changed quite a bit, but it's still a small town on Lake Erie. As you read this book, you'll encounter a lot of people, so it might help to have some background on my family, or at least my siblings.

- Me, Richard: I'm the youngest of four kids. Back then, there were a lot of Richards, but almost all of them went by Dick. I was no exception. I was Dick or Dickie until adulthood. By then, nobody wanted to go by that name.

So I made the change to Richard. But in this book, I'm Dick or Dickie.

- Jeff: My brother who is a year and a half older than me, but one year ahead in school.
- Cathy: My sister, second oldest in the family. She's about four years older than me.
- Pat: My other sister, and the oldest. She's about six years older than me.
- Dad (Warren): Dad was 28 years older than me.
- Mom (Thecla): Mom was 29 years older than me. And yes, her name really was "Thecla." There's not a lot of "Thecla's" around.

Dad, Mom, and Cathy have all passed. But in this book, they're still kinda alive. Which I like.

Even though our ages are scattered, between Jeff's birthday in January and Cathy's birthday in June, we are "every other year." Dad used to get a kick out of telling people that "We have four kids, ages of two, four, six, and eight," or "five, seven, nine, and eleven."

That doesn't have as much ring to it now that we're older. For instance, saying we're "66, 68, 70, and 72" doesn't sound quite as cool. Also, sadly, we lost Cathy about two years ago. I guess we'll retire the "every other year" idea.

So that's my family. You'll meet them more as you read!

Age 5 and 6

The Times That Built Me

While I tell a lot of stories of the 1960s, it's hard for people who didn't live through them to imagine just how different a time that was. For starters, there were a *lot* more kids. Today, the average family has one or two children. Maybe three. In the 60s, almost every family had at least three. Four or five kids was common, and some families had ten or more. Because of this, there were a lot more kids in every neighborhood. There were a lot more kids in school, and there were a lot more kids in things like Sunday school. So there was always someone to play with.

Unlike today, there were very few organized activities for kids. Sure, there was Little League for baseball, but that only lasted about eight to ten weeks at most, and it didn't start until about age eight. There was no soccer, no mini football, no biddy wrestling, no fall ball. Almost nobody took music, art, dance, or any other type of class outside of school, although piano lessons were common. Also, girls didn't do sports—just boys. There were no computers or video games, so normally, being inside was boring. We spent most of our playtime outside. The point of this is that as kids, we had a lot of free time, and a lot of kids to spend it with. So we played. If we wanted to play baseball, we didn't have lined fields, umpires, or uniforms. We just picked sides and played in the backyard. We'd use anything we could find for bases, and the field wasn't always complete. We commonly had driveways or garages or gardens in the way to work around. And because we didn't have nine kids per team, we'd designate right field as an out if you hit it there. Or we had shadow base runners. We got pretty creative.

Also, I don't know whether the world was safer then, or we just weren't as aware of the dangers. But we had so much freedom during playtime. Moms never seemed to worry that we'd be abducted or something evil like that.

I don't blame parents today for keeping a closer rein on their kids. And I don't blame parents for having their kids in all sorts of organized activities. But we didn't have those, and everything was great.

I'm not saying those times were better. I *am* saying they were different. The life my grandkids lead is nothing like my life as a kid. Better or worse? I have no idea. In this book, I describe the world as it was.

I'm Never Going to Grow Up

Dick sitting next to the counter, with Mom and Grandpa Clarence behind

As the youngest of four children, I was the baby of the family. It seemed like my siblings never failed to remind me of that.

I was little. And I was pretty sure I was always going to be little. Yes, my parents told me that someday I'd be big and tall, and maybe be a dad myself. I suppose I believed them. But believing something is true, and actually feeling it's true, are two different things.

I'M NEVER GOING TO GROW UP

Part of me was convinced I'd always be little. That I would never really grow. I know that seems stupid, but remember back when you were a kid. It was *forever* between one Christmas and the next. If your birthday was a week away, it seemed it took a loooong time to arrive. Time moves more slowly for little kids. So when I was five, it felt like I had been five forever. I wasn't 100 percent convinced my parents were telling me the truth about growing up.

Maybe, just maybe, they were hiding the truth, and I'd always be five. Honestly, I wondered. I was always waiting for some sign, some proof, one way or the other.

Now, there are a few perks that come with being the youngest. Not many, but some. And one is that you can fit in places your older siblings can't. For instance, I was the only one in the family who could walk under the counter in our kitchen while standing upright.

I know that isn't a huge thing, but I thought it was kinda cool for some reason. But one day, I went to walk under that counter, and *bam!* I hit my head. On the counter. Yep. I couldn't do it anymore. Which meant *I had grown*. Just like my parents told me I would.

In that one moment, I knew my parents were telling me the truth. I was actually going to grow up. I had just proven it by hitting my head on the counter.

It was a little thing, but it showed me a lot. Looking back, it was the first time I really knew I actually was growing up. That someday I'd be older. That life would change, that I wouldn't always be a little kid. In that one moment when I hit my head, my whole outlook on my long life ahead changed. Significantly. Over sixty years later, I still remember that moment. Because I really did grow up. I did become a dad. And all those things my parents told me would happen, happened.

My parents were telling the truth after all!

Alien

"Alien" is a common word. We all know what it means. But while most people today think of it as describing someone from another country, when I was a kid, it only meant someone from another planet. At least that's what it meant to me.

That was because I read comic books. We all did. I don't remember where we got them. Green's Drug Store, probably. They always had a lot of cool stuff. Did we buy them ourselves? I have no idea. I mean, none of us kids had any money. But somehow, we had them.

My favorite comic book was *Superman*. I loved the stories. In one comic he was fighting aliens from another planet. I still remember sitting on the back step, reading that comic book. It was a typical summer day. I was five or six, with, looking back on it, not a care in the world. When you're five, summer seems to last forever. One warm sunny day becomes another, on and on, with school and cold weather seemingly forever away.

Another point of interest is the back step I was sitting on. It's the same back step I have today. While I was raised mostly in that house, Mom and Dad built a new house a few blocks away (in the "new" section) when I was twelve. Well, high school, college, career, family, etc. took up about forty-five years or so, but after many, many twists and turns, at about the age of sixty, I ended up right back in the same place, living in the house I grew up in. I sleep in the same bedroom as when I was five, except instead of sharing a bed with my brother, I share it with my wife. So while these stories are memories, for many of them, I can picture exact details, because I'm still here.

We've remodeled and changed many things, but that back step is still there. Yes, it looks a little different, and no, I don't fit on it quite as well. But it's still there. And I can picture exactly what that summer day must have been like.

I was sitting on the brick steps. I'm almost positive I was wearing tennis shoes (or "sneakers" for those on the East Coast), shorts, and a white T-shirt. That's what I always wore. (Nothing much has changed in sixty years—that's still my normal clothing, except the T-shirt is now gray.) While I was sitting there reading, Davey, from across the street, came by, and we started talking.

Davey, being older, was wiser than me. He walked up and said, "Hey Dickie, what are you reading?"

"Superman," I responded.

"What's it about?"

"Well, he's fighting these aliens from another planet. Superman is hiding from them for some reason, and he's worried because his cape is sticking out. But the aliens didn't even see him. It turns out these aliens can't see the color red. So I guess Superman got lucky."

As I was explaining this, Davey started laughing. He laughed more and more, the more I told the story.

Finally, I asked, "What's so funny?"

Davey said, "You're saying it wrong."

"What am I saying wrong? Superman?"

"No, Superman is right. It's 'alien' you're not saying right."

I had pronounced it *a-LEE-an*, with a short *a* and the accent on the second syllable. But Davey said it was pronounced with a long *a*, and the accent on the first syllable: *A-lee-an*.

I now pronounce it correctly. I learned. But I still remember that day. Davey wasn't really laughing at me; he just thought it was funny. He didn't make fun of me or anything. He was actually being helpful. Somehow, that stuck with me.

Even today, whenever I see that word, I think of that warm summer day, reading comic books on the back step. When life was simple, and all I had to do was read a comic book.

Mom, Where Were You?

All her adult life, Mom was a nurse. She worked at the local hospital. I knew that, of course. But it seemed like she was always home. When did she work? As a little kid, I didn't think about that. Until one day.

It was early morning, probably around 7:30 or so. It must have been summer, or a Saturday, because I was home, not at school. For some reason I was looking out the front window. I remember seeing Mom dressed in white, from her nurse's cap all the way down to her white shoes. That's what nurses wore back then. And she was out walking. Walking! Why? And why was she in her nurse's uniform? You'd think I would have asked her why she was out for a walk. Maybe I did. But if so, she didn't really give me a straight answer.

Well, not until many years later. When I was older, I told her about that memory, and she started laughing. She said, "We had four kids, and your dad didn't make enough money to support the family with just his salary. So I worked at the hospital. But we couldn't afford childcare, so I worked nights. Another nurse and I shared a full-time position. We each worked every other night, eleven to seven. So when you saw me, I was walking home from my shift."

Let's parse that just a bit, okay?

One: She was *walking* home. Because she didn't have her driver's license yet. She walked the mile to and from the hospital. Rain or shine. Snow or sleet. Does anyone do that today? Not many.

Two: She never told us. Or at least she didn't tell us boys. My sisters, being older, probably knew. But Jeff and I had no idea. She said she thought we might be afraid if we knew she was gone. And she was probably right.

Three: When did she sleep? I asked her. She told me that those nights, she just didn't. She said she could normally get a nap in sometime during the day, probably when us little kids were taking our naps.

I find it mind-boggling. Working three or four nights a week, walking both ways, and not sleeping those nights.

Many times in my life, I've been so busy with work, family, and life in general that I was completely dog-tired, worn out, exhausted. But as hard as I worked, as busy as I was, I didn't work all night, then come home and take care of four kids. That's way beyond anything I've done. And way beyond what most of us have ever done. Yet Mom did it. Like it was a regular thing.

Every time I think about that, I'm amazed all over again.

JoJo

JoJo

Mom was your typical 50s-60s mother. She had four kids, worked as a nurse, and did all the cooking and cleaning. She got zero help with any of that from Dad. Not that Dad was bad, but it was the 50s and 60s. Men didn't normally do "women's work." And Dad worked…all the time. Mom pretty much raised us all by herself.

Mothers of that era were really something with all they had to do. Mom was no exception. Still, there came times when she was overwhelmed. Our next-door neighbor, Josephine, really made our lives better. We called her JoJo. Whether everyone called her that or just us kids did, I have no idea. She was the "old lady next door" who was just…wonderful.

Actually, she wasn't that old. When we met her, she was in her early fifties. But it seemed old at the time. She apparently loved us kids. And we really loved her back. We knew we could go over to JoJo's any time we wanted, invited or not, and she'd always be nice to us.

Sometimes we'd help her in the garden. (We thought we were helping, but you never know.) Sometimes we'd help her in the kitchen. Somehow, she always seemed to know when Mom was at her wits' end. She'd stop over and tell Mom to "go take some time, do whatever you want. I'll watch them for a while."

Honestly, every kid growing up, and every parent of those kids, should have a JoJo. I have nothing but good memories. For instance, her oven had a window in it, like they all do now. But Mom's didn't. So you couldn't see things cook. I remember sitting in front of JoJo's oven on one of those oval knitted rugs that were so common back then, watching cookies bake. I always imagined I was in a boat, looking out the window. I'm not sure why I thought cookies baking had anything to do with boats, but hey, I was a little kid with an active imagination.

One time, my sister Pat was helping JoJo with something. Pat came running home, saying, "Mom, I'm helping JoJo clean, and she says I need more elbow grease. Do we have any elbow grease?" (Pat has always been a little gullible!)

My brother's cat Cookie used to leave his droppings right next to a particular flower in her garden. Instead of complaining, she called it the "Cookie potty plant." She wasn't mad at all. She was so good to us, and so good to Mom. She never got mad.

Until one day. My brother and I went over to her front porch, and for some reason, we smeared mud all over it. I have no idea why. We loved JoJo, so we weren't trying to be mean or nasty. But we did it. When JoJo came out, it was probably the only time I ever saw her upset. She made us clean it up, which we understood. And then she said we weren't allowed in her yard for a week. A whole week! It decimated us.

Years later, I saw a picture of Jeff and I on the front sidewalk on a huge tricycle we had, right at our property's edge, staring longingly into JoJo's yard. We weren't allowed in. While it hurt us to be banished, I'm sure it hurt JoJo just as much. But she stood by it, and we really did learn our lesson.

Which is why it was so devastating when the very bad day came. That day, I came home from first grade and saw an ambulance next door. JoJo had had a heart attack. And she didn't make it. We were all heartbroken, as you can imagine.

Jeff remembers that day because it was the day he "learned to write cursive." He wanted to come right home and tell JoJo all about it. But he never got the chance. It was one of the worst days of our young lives.

    Looking back, JoJo wasn't old at all. She died at fifty-seven. I'm much older than that now. But she only had one child, and by the time I was born, he was already an adult with a family of his own.

    Maybe she missed kids. Maybe she was just naturally nice. All I know is that she made a big impact on all of us kids by being nice and treating us like we were special. I know Mom appreciated her so much. She was that big a help to a young mom with four kids.

    My childhood was better because of JoJo. I feel bad for kids who don't have a JoJo living next door. She was a blessing, to us kids and to Mom.

    To this day, I still miss her.

Andy. And Dandy.

Cathy and Dick, with Andy

Do little girls still play with dolls? I'm sure they do. How about boys? Do they?

In today's world, I know a lot of parents try not to pigeonhole their kids as far as what they play with. For instance, I know a three-year-old boy who likes to play in the kitchen. So his parents bought him a kid's play kitchen with all the accessories. He loves it.

Sixty years ago, that probably would not have happened. Back then, we bought boys footballs, baseball mitts, and trucks, and for girls, it was Easy-Bake Ovens, dolls, and just about anything pink. But times have changed, pretty sure. While boys are still different from girls, I don't think their playthings are quite as gender-structured as they were back then.

The reason I'm bringing this up is because both my brother and I had dolls. Of course, we didn't call them "dolls." They were friends we hung out with. More like Hobbes from *Calvin and Hobbes* than Barbie. Jeff's was a little plastic doll, probably about ten inches tall, named Billy Boy. And I had a Raggedy Andy, which I called, of course, Andy.

We played with those guys quite a bit. I'm guessing my dad was secretly worried. In those days, it was definitely "boys will be boys." If not, dads were concerned.

But I had Andy, and I carried him around with me all the time. One day, Jeff and I were taking a bath. I don't know if brothers still take baths together, but back then, it saved time and money. We used to take baths together all the time. And Jeff decided to bring Billy Boy into the bath with him. Well, if he could, so could I. So I brought Andy into the bath.

Of course, that was a bit problematic. While Billy Boy was plastic, Andy was fabric, stuffed with "stuff." It didn't hurt Billy Boy to get wet, but it did a number on Andy. He was completely soaked. When Mom saw him, she wasn't sure what to do. Probably the best thing would've been to just let him dry out. But I'm guessing I was probably really upset, and wanted Andy back to normal *right now!* So she put him in the dryer.

That sounds good. Except it wasn't. I remember watching Andy flopping around in the dryer and all his hair was falling out. I watched in horror, screaming, "You killed Andy! You killed Andy!"

That was certainly traumatic, so Mom did the best she could. She stopped the dryer and took Andy out. Of course, he was still soaking wet. But Mom remembered Jo-Jo had a clothesline in her basement. (Not everyone had dryers back then.) Jo-Jo told her she could hang Andy in her basement. So we did. It took a few days for him to dry out completely. I went over there a couple times to say hi as he was drying out.

Eventually, Andy did dry out. But he wasn't the same. Most of his hair was gone. He looked pretty bad. Sometime shortly after that, Mom bought me a new Andy to replace the old one. But Andy was still…Andy. Yes, he looked horrible. Yes, he had lost most of his hair. But Mom hadn't killed him after all. Instead of getting a replacement friend, I now had two. I had Andy, and I had his new friend, which I called "Dandy." Andy and Dandy. It was perfect.

I don't know how much longer I played with Andy and Dandy. I eventually grew out of them. Years later, when I was probably in elementary school, I found them stored away. I got them back out and put them in my bedroom. I told Mom it was "just because," like it was no big deal. But secretly, even at the advanced age of eight or nine, it gave me comfort to have my old friends with me. I was happy to have my friends back. Just don't call them dolls.

ANDY. AND DANDY.

Years and years after this, when I was an adult with kids of my own, I heard a song from *Toy Story 2* called "When She Loved Me." It was sung by a doll that had belonged to a little girl. As the girl grew up, she didn't need her little doll anymore. As you probably know, the toys in the *Toy Story* series are conscious. The little doll was heartbroken that she was stuffed in a box, unused and unloved. This song reminded me of growing out of Andy and Dandy. The doll in the movie was so sad. Which is why it bothers me that I can no longer find Andy and Dandy. I've looked everywhere, but no luck. And I have no memory of getting rid of them. I'd never have thrown them away, yet they seem to be…nowhere.

I just hope Andy and Dandy aren't upset. Wherever they are, I hope they know I still love them, miss them, and think about them from time to time. I like to think some other little boy has them now, and he loves them as much as I did. They would love that.

My Toy Guns

When we were kids, we all had toy guns. We played cops and robbers, and cowboys and Indians. Or we'd pretend we were Americans against Germans in WWII. In our minds, cops, cowboys, and Americans were good. Robbers, Indians, and Germans were bad. Luckily, as we grew up, we realized those were stereotypes, and not accurate.

These were toy guns of course, and they didn't shoot anything. Some used caps to make a loud sound. Caps were little spots of gunpowder that came on a paper roll. You'd feed the roll into the gun, and when you pulled the trigger, the hammer came down and hit that spot of gunpowder, making a "pop" noise. It wasn't anything like a real gun, but it was still cool. We didn't do that often though, because that meant we'd have to keep buying more caps. And we were kids—none of us had any money.

Mostly we used the guns as props. If we didn't have a toy gun, we'd use a stick, a finger, or anything we could find. As long as we could point it at someone and yell "Bang!" it worked.

The most fun part, actually, wasn't shooting someone. It was getting shot. Because of TV, I guess, we assumed that whenever someone was shot, they'd clutch their heart, fall back on the ground, and lay spreadeagle. Then they'd raise their head and have a few "last words" before their head rolled to the side. Only then would they be "dead." So that's how we "died." Every time. I'm not pretending there was anything realistic about it. I think we even knew that's not how it always happened. But we saw it on TV, and it was fun. So we did it.

When I was really little, Mom wouldn't let me have a toy gun. She said I wasn't old enough. When my sixth birthday came around, she finally told me I could get a toy gun.

This was huge! I couldn't wait. Really. When my birthday came, it was time. Mom and I went up to the dime store.

This was 1961. There was no Walmart. No Home Depot. No chain stores of any kind, as far as I know. In fact, in Port Clinton, there were no big stores at all. Sure, stores like Sears and JCPenney existed. But not in our town. The biggest store probably was my dad's TV and appliance store, and that would be considered tiny compared to today's stores.

Honestly, that was okay. Port Clinton had almost anything you wanted. We had shoe stores, drugstores, clothing stores, restaurants, bars, bakeries, grocery stores, lumber stores, corner markets, banks, gas stations, jewelry stores, photo stores, a theater, and more. Most were concentrated in our downtown area. On special occasions, we went to Sandusky, a nearby bigger town, or even Toledo, a huge city. But those times were rare. Although I have to admit I loved going with Mom to Sandusky, because a couple stores there had escalators. That was pretty cool.

For the most part, though, all our shopping was done in Port Clinton. When I wanted a toy gun, we had two choices: W.R. Thomas and Ben Franklin. Both were considered "dime stores." That doesn't mean everything was a dime, of course. Think of them as tiny Walmarts. They had just about anything you could want, except groceries. W.R. Thomas even had a candy counter, which was pretty neat. For this trip, mom chose W.R. Thomas, because it had a bigger toy section.

I remember walking in and going all the way to the back, on the right, to the toy section. There, against the wall, was the gun display. Today, toy guns look like toy guns. They're required to have orange barrels so we know they're not real. But back then, they looked like real guns. Okay, not to someone who really knew guns, of course. But to a kid, they looked just like real guns.

There were a bunch of them. I was thinking about a toy rifle so I could be like The Rifleman, from the TV show with the same name. But Mom told me a handgun would be better; since it was smaller, I'd probably use it more. So that narrowed it down a bit. I knew I didn't want a modern gun. I wanted a gun like cowboys used to use on the westerns. It had to have a holster and gun belt.

Well, I'll tell you, I hit the jackpot. Not only did I find exactly what I was looking for; the gun I bought was actually a *pair* of guns. Six-shooters with revolving barrels. And *two* holsters, one for each hip. I was so excited I wore them home with me.

I felt like the coolest kid on the block. While all the bigger kids had toy guns, nobody but me had *two*. Because I had two holsters, I could wear the guns with the grip pointing backward like Marshal Dillon. Or I could put them in the holsters backward, with the grip facing forward, like Bat Masterson. Or even one of each. It was my chance to be cool.

And yes, my guns used caps, when we had them. On special occasions, I had a few rolls of caps for my guns.

I loved those guns. Not because I was a crazed lunatic who liked to kill things. After all, we knew it was just pretend. I loved them because they made me feel old. In my mind, I had graduated into a new club where I was old enough to have toy guns. And kids always like to feel older. So this was pretty cool.

Besides that, cops and robbers got a lot more fun!

Family Photo

My mom and dad decided we needed a picture of all four kids. Not just a picture, but a portrait.

In the days before smartphones and digital cameras, this was a pretty big deal. Sure, we could take the picture ourselves. We did that once in a while, mostly for special occasions. But it wasn't the same as going to a real studio, with a real photographer and a real camera. The resulting picture was so much better than anything we could do ourselves, so my parents made an appointment for our sitting.

I'll be honest—I don't remember much of the process, but I remember the result. A few years later, when I looked at that picture, it looked like the younger me was crying. It sure seemed like it anyway. So I asked Mom.

Well, she reiterated how big a deal it was to get a family portrait. We all got dressed up in our church clothes and went downtown to Misch's Photo Studio. Mr. Misch spent considerable time getting everything set up just right. I was the youngest, so I'm sure I was bored. But finally, after he had the camera, lights, and everything else set up, he got us four kids arranged. All went well, apparently, till he said "Okay, now I'm going to shoot the picture."

FAMILY PHOTO

According to Mom, all I heard was the word "shoot." So I thought he was going to shoot us. And no amount of explanation could convince me otherwise.

So I cried, and wouldn't stop.

Needless to say, he didn't shoot me. I'm still here. But there is no way anyone could convince five-year-old me. Until it was all done, and we were on our way home.

I was still alive. But in the picture, I definitely was crying!

Mom's Wisdom, Part 1

Mom in her kitchen

One time, our whole family was eating hot dogs in the living room. Yes, in the living room. I have no idea what the occasion was; we almost never ate in the living room. There must have been something special on TV, because I vividly remember sitting on the floor eating a hot dog. But that's not the story here. The story is what happened when I finished that hot dog.

Back in the 60s, there was no "open concept." The kitchen was a separate room, and Mom, like most moms, spent a whole lot of time there, while the rest of the family was elsewhere. Looking back, I wonder how much family life moms in the 50s and 60s missed because they were always in the kitchen. Of course, they never complained. At least Mom didn't, I don't think. It was expected, and they did their duties. While I'm sure they would have liked to sit with the family, I think they were somewhat okay with it, for the most part. After all, they were providing for their family.

So when we were eating in the living room, of course Mom was in the kitchen, still preparing food maybe, or doing dishes, or whatever.

When I finished my hot dog, I wanted another one. I took my plate back to the kitchen and said, "Mom, can I have another one?"

Well, she looked at me and said, "I'm sorry, but we don't have any more." Before I could process that and get upset, she added, "But I've got something even better for you." She went to the refrigerator, took out the bologna, put a slice in a pan, and fried it. When it was done, she rolled it up and put it in a bun (so it kinda looked like a hot dog) and said, "Here, this is better. But don't tell anyone. They'll all be jealous."

I took my new treat back into the living room and ate my "hot dog." Was I beaming with pride and happiness? Did I feel extra special? Did I keep it a secret, just between Mom and me?

Yes, yes, and yes.

To a kid, Mom is just Mom. But as I grew older, I realized the wisdom she had. This was just one example that has stayed with me all these years. I raised two kids of my own, and I was *not* an absent father. Especially in the summer, when I was on vacation from my teaching job, I was with them all the time. But honestly, I'm not sure I had the wisdom Mom had. I don't know if I would have handled this like she did. I like to think so, but really I don't know. Mom had a wisdom I don't think I ever matched. Hopefully my kids don't realize that!

Telling Time

The clock I learned to tell time on

It's tough being a kid. They have so much to learn. From as soon as they can talk, and even sometimes before that, parents have a whole list of things to teach them. Read? First you have to learn your ABCs. Count? Yeah, that too. How about tying your shoes? Telling time? Counting money? And on and on. A whole lot for a little kid to learn. But of course, we all have to. And we all do. Eventually.

TALES FROM THE HUMP

I learned pretty quickly as a kid. At least that's what Mom told me. Of course, is any mom ever going to tell her kid anything different? Doubtful. So maybe I was a quick learner. But then again, maybe not.

Some things were easy. The alphabet was just memorizing. Reading, of course, was much harder, but I handled that okay. Counting was pretty simple. Well, at least one to ten. It got a little tricky once I hit eleven! After thirty, it got easier again, because the thirties were just like the twenties.

But some things just didn't make sense. At least to me. Take money, for instance. Okay, a penny is one cent, and a nickel is five cents. Fine. But then you hit the dime. Wait, it's worth *more* than a penny? And *more* than a nickel? How can that be? It's so tiny. Yet it is. A quarter is worth more yet, but it's big. So that's all okay. But paper money? Really, how can this piece of paper be worth more than this shiny quarter? I mean a quarter is worth twenty-five pennies, and a dollar bill is worth a hundred? None of that made sense to me.

Then there's telling time. Yeah, good luck. Today, most clocks are digital. I know some kids and teens can't tell time on a clock. Not because they're stupid, but because they've never had to. Kinda like asking a twelve-year-old to dial a rotary phone. Or asking anyone how to start a 1918 Model T. We no longer have these skills known to previous generations.

When I was a kid, digital was not a thing. So we had to learn to tell time. And it was quite a process. The big hand is for the minutes; the little hand is for the hour. Why? Isn't an hour bigger than a minute? So why isn't the big hand the hour? That made no sense. But also, to me, the hour hand seemed bigger. Yes, I know it's shorter, but it usually *is* fatter. At least it was on our clock. So when someone said "the big hand," I looked at the short fat one, not the long skinny one. Which caused all kinds of confusion when I was learning. Once Mom realized my mistake, we made it work. But it took a while. Honestly, to this day, I still think the hour hand is bigger. At least on some clocks.

The one that really got me was "a quarter after." I understood things like "eight thirty." Or "eleven o'clock." After all, we played hide and seek, and when we were "it", we had to hide our eyes and count by fives. "Five, ten, fifteen, twenty…" (We kinda sang it.) So when we learned that the numbers on the clock were counting by fives, that was okay. But then came "a quarter after seven." Okay, we all know that means 7:15. That's pretty obvious to most of us. Because of course a quarter of an hour is fifteen minutes.

But to a kid, a quarter is just a piece of money. A five-year-old doesn't know fractions. (At least I didn't, no matter how quick a learner Mom told me I was.) So to me, "a quarter after seven" meant 7:25. I mean, why not? If a quarter is worth twenty-five cents, then "a quarter after seven" should mean twenty-five minutes after seven.

It doesn't. I know that now. But for way longer than I should have, I thought "a quarter after" meant "twenty-five minutes after." Not "fifteen minutes after." I was telling time wrong for quite a while. And always being late, or early, or something.

I can't believe I was the only kid who thought that. I've asked a few people, and none of them remember having that problem. Either they were smarter than I was, or they can't remember.

As adults, we mostly forget how our brains worked when we were little. When we're teaching our kids money one day, we don't realize that "a quarter is twenty-five cents" is going to conflict with the "quarter after seven" situation the next day. But it does. At least it did to me.

Maybe I wasn't as quick a learner as Mom told me. *Or maybe I was so good that I put things together that other kids didn't.* Yeah, I doubt that.

I'm choosing to believe it anyway. Just in defense of my five-year-old self.

All Adult Men Are Named Warren

My dad's name was Warren. Of course, I just knew him as "Dad."

But somehow, I figured out he had another name. Probably because Mom called him that I suppose. Somehow, at some time, I figured out his name was Warren.

Of course, I thought my dad was old. Now, he was only twenty-eight when I was born, so when I was a little kid of five or six, he was in his early thirties. Definitely *not* old. But to a five-year-old, yeah, that's pretty ancient.

Our next-door neighbor was also old. Looking back on it, he probably was much older than Dad. But to me, all adults were old.

The funny thing about our neighbor was that his name was also Warren. Just a coincidence of course. But to me as a little kid, I didn't think it was a coincidence at all. I just figured that all old men were named Warren.

No, it doesn't make sense, and no, it's not logical. Especially since our other neighbor JoJo had a husband named Ralph. Somehow that didn't register though. For quite a while, I thought "Warren" was what all old men were called.

Sometimes I was a very bright kid. But sometimes, not so much.

How Did She Know?

When I was little, Mom did a lot of ironing. All moms did. "Permanent press" wasn't invented till the mid-60s. So Mom ironed. All the time. Dad ran a business, which meant he wore a shirt, coat, and tie to work every day. So there was a *lot* of ironing. Dads *never* ironed. Back in those days, it was considered "women's work."

When I was older and living on my own, I asked Mom some questions about ironing. Specifically, I wanted to know how she dealt with shirts that needed to be hung up. She told me that after ironing, she put them on the hanger and buttoned the top two buttons, and then every other one.

I was flabbergasted. I mean, now, when I wash and dry a dress shirt (an extremely rare event), I pull it out of the dryer, put it on the hanger, and button *one* button. Maybe two if I'm feeling energized. But she had to iron every single shirt, which took long enough. Then she buttoned all those buttons! Nope, I never did anything like that.

Back to the past: it's not surprising that I remember Mom ironing. It was one of her biggest (and most hated) chores. She always did it in the same place. She had her ironing board set up semi-permanently in the laundry room, just off the kitchen. I walked by it all the time. To me, it was just part of the surroundings, I guess.

One time I walked by it, and I noticed something that looked wrong. The iron was sitting up on its heel, its point in the air. Which, of course, is how we set an iron when we're not using it. I know that now. But that time I walked by it, I remember thinking that when Mom was ironing, the flat (hot) side was down. When I saw the iron standing up, it just looked...wrong. Because I was trying to be helpful, I set the iron down flat. And walked away. Happy I could help put things right.

Well, the trouble was that the iron was on. So when I set it down, it burned a hole through the ironing board cover and down into the padding. When Mom went back into the room, she saw the iron smoking, and her ironing board cover was ruined. And she was mad!

Very soon, I heard Mom yell, "All you kids get in here. Right now!"

We could tell she was mad. Really mad. She didn't get mad often, but when she did, we knew it. So we all ran into the laundry room. Right away. We lined up from oldest (Pat) to youngest (me). She said, "Who did this? Tell me right now!"

Pat said, "It wasn't me."

Cathy echoed, "Not me."

Jeff looked surprised, wondering how anyone could be so stupid. He also responded, "It wasn't me."

Then Mom looked at me. I knew I was going to be in big trouble, because Mom was really, really mad. Normally, I was an honest kid. But she was so mad; there was no way I was going to admit it. So I lied, and said, "It wasn't me."

Somehow, she knew anyway. She walked over to me, put me over her knee, and paddled me right there on the spot.

I couldn't figure out how she knew. But I was just a little kid, and I'm sure guilt was written all over my face. While Mom was very wise, she probably didn't have to be a genius to figure out who the guilty party was.

The thing was, I wasn't trying to be bad. Actually, I was trying to be good. I really thought the iron was sitting wrong, and I really thought I was helping. I had no idea the iron would burn a hole into the fabric. I just thought that it looked wrong, so I fixed it.

I wonder what Mom would have done if I had come clean and told her the truth, that I was trying to help. Mom was a reasonable person. She probably still would have been mad, but I'm guessing she would have tempered her anger with a little bit of wisdom and explained to me why what I did was wrong.

I was way too scared at the time to think of anything like that. I just tried to lie my way out of it.

That was the wrong choice!

Cookie

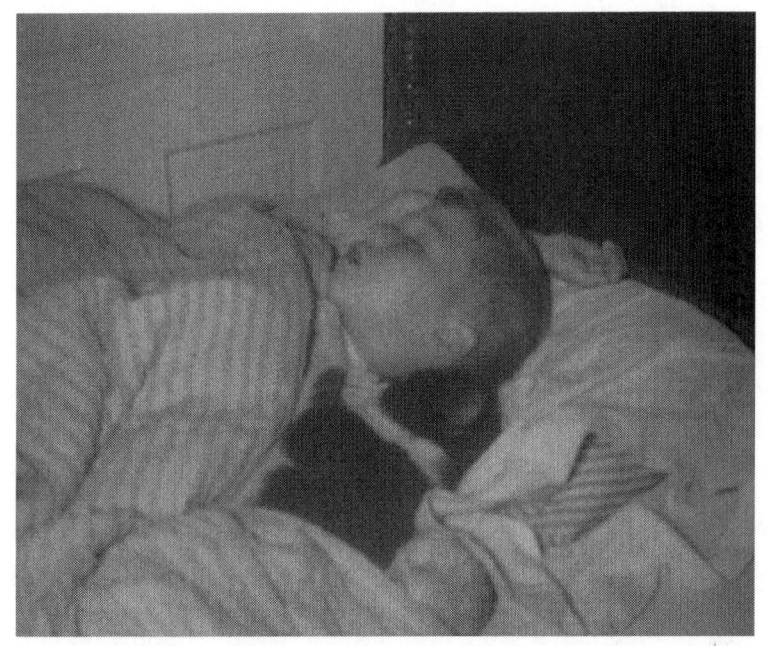

Jeff sleeping with Cookie and Billy Boy

Cookie was my brother's cat, a black and white tomcat Jeff loved. I have no idea how it came about that Jeff, not the entire family, had a cat. But he did. I'm guessing he got it when we had a dog called Peaches. Mind you, I have no recollection of Peaches, except every night when Mom said our prayers with us, it started with "Now I lay me down to sleep" and ended with "God bless Peaches and Cookie." You'd think that would have confused me, because yes, we had a cat named Cookie. But we didn't have a dog. At least not then. Apparently, we'd had Peaches earlier, but we kept saying his (or her) name in our prayers long after he (or she) was gone. That was just a part of the whole prayer. We said it every night, because it was a habit, and Mom told us to. That didn't mean it made a lot of sense. I never put it together that I was praying for a dead dog. Realistically, it's probably better we didn't think too much about what we were saying. If we had, the "If I die before I wake" part would definitely have freaked me out!

Back then, a lot of us had dogs and cats, but for the most part, we didn't fence in the yards or put them on leashes, although a few people did. We didn't really take them for walks either. Nope. Our cats just roamed the neighborhood, doing cat things. The dogs were the same. If the dog wanted out, we opened the door and let him go. I know we can never go back to those days, because there were significant problems. But for the pet at the time, it was great.

So Cookie was a neighborhood cat. Yes, he slept inside, and of course we fed him. But he came and went pretty much as he pleased. We didn't worry about where he (or the dog) did his business. He just went…somewhere. In those days, cat poop or dog poop was part of your world. If a dog owner from back then could see dog owners now? Taking the dog for a walk on a leash and picking up the droppings with plastic bags? That dog owner from the past would be amazed. Those things didn't happen in the 60s.

Honestly, as much as we dote on our pets today, sixty years ago was a great time to be a family pet. The run of the neighborhood was guaranteed. What a life!

Back to Cookie. I don't remember a whole lot about him, except he was male, black and white, and not neutered. In those days, it was common to "fix" a female pet, but for male pets we mostly didn't bother. I'm not sure when that became common. Because he wasn't neutered, and because he was a tomcat, he roamed a lot. (We never asked him where he went, or who he was meeting.) But one day Cookie was not acting like he should, and he smelled pretty bad. Mom took him to the vet. She was told he had some kidney disease and it was terminal. I don't know how long he lasted, but eventually, Cookie died.

While I don't remember much about Cookie's sickness, I vividly remember my brother's reaction. Remember, Cookie was Jeff's cat. When Cookie died, Jeff was probably six or seven. And he didn't take it well.

Cookie had to be buried. Why Dad didn't do this, I have no idea, but I'm guessing he was working. I went out to the backyard to see if Jeff needed help, and there he was, digging a hole all the way to China, or at least it seemed like it. I remember him back in the corner of the garden, digging and digging and digging, tears streaming down his face. I swear the hole was eight feet deep. It was probably just a few feet deep. But it seemed like eight feet.

While we soon got another dog, Rusty, we never got another cat that I can remember. Not until Cathy brought home Eli, a cat she had kept in her dorm room. She brought him home for "just a while." Which meant for years. But except for Eli, we never had another cat. Jeff has had cats off and on over the years, but he still remembers Cookie, his first. While I don't remember Cookie well, I remember Jeff digging, with all the tears.

Over sixty years later, I've buried dogs and cats of my own. Just like Jeff, I had tears streaming down my face as well. Some things never change.

See You Next Year

Because first grade was over sixty years ago, I don't remember all that much about it. But I remember a few things.

I remember that we had two reading groups, and I was in the first one. The stories were about Alice and Jerry. I remember one boy in my class had much darker skin than any of my neighborhood friends. Weston was the first African-American I had ever known. He was also the funniest kid I'd ever met. He always seemed to make us all laugh. I remember that Mrs. Manz was my teacher. And I remember that two different girls kissed me! (More on that later.)

One event I *really* remember is our trip to the zoo. Actually, I remember looking forward to it much more than the trip itself. It was a tradition that on the last day of school, all the first-grade students and teachers went to the Toledo Zoo. It was a big deal, and we all looked forward to it. I even remember what clothes I wore—Mom had bought me a special outfit. It was a red and white striped shirt and matching red beachcomber pants. I was definitely going to be the coolest kid at the zoo.

I remember another thing. It was sometime in the middle of the school year, and as we were leaving for the day, Mrs. Manz said to all of us: "See you next year."

Wait, what? Next year? That can't be. We *all* knew we went to the zoo on the last day of school. How could she be talking about "next year" if we hadn't gone to the zoo yet? Had they canceled the zoo this year? Was I already done with first grade? What was I missing? As you can imagine, I was very upset.

Once I got home and told Mom, it all made sense. This random day in the middle of the school year wasn't just any random day. It was the last day before Christmas vacation. Which meant that when we came back after vacation, 1961 would be 1962. The "See you next year" comment now made sense.

Apparently all that information was just too much for me at first. All I could think about was that I had missed the trip to the zoo!

I've often wondered, in the years since, whether Mrs. Manz knew she was messing with us. Or if she didn't realize little kids would misinterpret what she said. Of course, maybe everyone else figured it out but me. That is certainly possible.

Maybe I wasn't quite as smart as I thought I was.

The Birds and the Bees

We don't normally expect a first-grade kid to understand much about the birds and the bees. I was no exception. However, I remember two incidents very vividly, probably because they were on this particular subject.

The first happened one evening when Mom and Dad had some friends over. They were all sitting around the living room, talking and talking, like adults always seemed to do. Us kids were supposed to be somewhere else doing something else. But I walked through the living room and I heard a conversation that wasn't meant for me.

One of the women said, "Did you hear about Julie? She's pregnant!" Julie was a neighbor girl who was nineteen and unmarried.

"I know," Mom responded. "And her dad is really, really mad at her."

This confused me. At the age of five, I assumed that once people got married, they just kinda became pregnant. It was a natural thing that just happened. I didn't realize there was any more to it than that. I couldn't understand how she could have become pregnant, because she wasn't married. That made no sense. But even more confusing was why her dad would be mad. I asked Mom, "Why is her dad mad? I don't get it."

"It's a kinda confusing thing," Mom replied. "But it's nothing you have to worry about."

And that was that. I didn't really give it much more thought.

Until one day just a bit later. Some of us neighborhood kids were playing the board game Life in our backyard. If you don't remember that game, each person had a car, used as a token. They spun a dial to see how many spaces to move. The goal was to get to the end first with as much money as possible. Depending on what spot you landed on, you could make money, lose money, buy a house, have kids, go to college, etc.

In this particular game, I kept landing on spaces that gave me more kids. Soon I had a bunch of kids in my car.

So far so good. Except playing with us in that game was John Larson. He was the neighborhood bad boy. Not really a bad kid, but he swore. A lot. He was the first person I ever heard say the f-word. And yes, we were in first grade. (I know because John moved away right after first grade.) For the most part, though, I was a good kid. His swearing didn't rub off on me. To his credit, he never pressured me to swear or do anything bad. He was just who he was, and didn't get upset when we weren't like him.

When I added still another child to my car during the game, he said something like, "You must be really busy!"

I had no idea what he meant. But then he said more, and to this day I remember it word for word. He looked at me and said, "You don't believe you have to fuck to have kids, do you?"

When he said it, somehow, in that instant, I knew he was right. At the ripe old age of five, I finally understood a bit more about the birds and the bees.

Of course, I had no idea what that really meant. In fact, I didn't understand it at all. But somehow I immediately knew that adults did something he described with the f-word.

I have no idea when the details became clear to me. It doesn't really matter. All I know is that John Larson taught me the facts of life, at the age of five, playing a board game in the backyard.

And I never told Mom or Dad!

A Whole Penny

One great aspect of being a kid in the 60s was that there was a lot of freedom. In the summer when school was out, we'd leave the house after breakfast and go out in the neighborhood to play. I have no idea what exactly we did, but we had friends across the street, down the alley, over on the next street, etc. There was a whole neighborhood of kids, and we went to somebody's yard and played.

The oldest kid was Davey, who lived right across the street. He was the same age as my sister Cathy, four years older than me. But for whatever reason, he hung out with us littler kids, and it somehow worked. Then there was Gordy, who lived close to Davey. He was a year older than me, and he could do a "snot-spit." He'd make this weird noise in his head, and then spit on the ground. As you can guess, it was a mix of snot and spit. Gross, yes. But we thought it was pretty neat. Johnny, who lived across the street from Gordy, was in my grade. He was really fast, and he was the coolest kid. I always wanted to be like him, but I was never that cool. Ricky moved in a few years later, and while a little older as well, we hung out a lot. And of course there was my brother Jeff, a year older than me.

There were a few others also. Davey's little sister, Mary Jane, was a year older than me. And Gigi, who lived right next door to Davey, was a couple years younger, so she never played with us. Finally, there was Tom Tom, but he was a little kid too, and he always sucked his thumb. Mary Jane, Gigi, and Tom Tom didn't play with us that much. It was normally Davey, Gordy, Johnny, Ricky, Jeff, and me. Sometimes other kids would join, but we were the main group.

We had a pretty big backyard. Or at least it seemed big to us. (Now, it seems so small.) When we played baseball, we used our yard. But sometimes we would play chase, a glorified version of tag. I hated it, because even though I was fast for my age, I was the youngest, so I had trouble catching anyone. When we played games like that, we started in Davey's yard. We could use the entire block and run anywhere we wanted.

I assume we all went home for lunch, but I don't remember any of that. I just remember running all over, having a great time. Mom didn't know exactly where we were, but back then it didn't seem to worry parents. If she needed us, she'd walk out the door and yell our names. We'd usually hear it and go home.

There was another benefit of all that freedom. There was a gas station just a two-minute walk away. We'd go out our back door, cross the backyard, walk down a couple of alleys, and we'd be at Kelly's, a tiny gas station. Gas stations back then didn't have convenience stores, but they usually had candy bars, and even penny candy. Deal!

I didn't go there a lot, because of course I never had any money. But one day, I was playing in the backyard, and I found a penny in the grass. A whole penny! It had obviously been hit by a lawnmower, because it had a big cut in it. But it was all there. I ran in the house and yelled to Mom, "I'm going to Kelly's!" I'm not sure why I told her; as I said, normally we just ran all over. I think I told her because I didn't know if the penny was still good. I mean, it was cut pretty bad. But she must have told me it was okay, because off to Kelly's I went.

I remember being so excited. What a windfall! A whole penny, to spend on just me! I know that seems odd, but to me as a little kid, it was a huge stroke of luck. I did go to Kelly's, and they accepted my penny, and I got my piece of candy.

It was a great day. It's not every day you find such a huge amount of money. No, a penny isn't really huge. I probably knew that. But it was a penny more than I'd had before I saw it, and it was worth a piece of candy. I felt very blessed that day.

Years later, in my thirties, I found a twenty-dollar bill. I was excited for that twenty dollars, just like I had been for the penny about thirty years earlier. I guess it wasn't really much different. Either way, both times I had an unexpected windfall. I still remember how happy I was finding that penny. And the twenty dollars.

What I wouldn't give to be able to be that happy just by finding a penny. It sure would make life simpler.

Piano Lessons

We were a musical family. Mom had played the trumpet in her youth, but she sold her trumpet for twenty-five dollars to buy her wedding dress, so she didn't have it anymore. Dad had a nice voice, but I'm pretty sure he only sang when he had a few too many. But we did have a piano. A very old, very large upright Stultz and Bauer piano. And we all took lessons. I don't know if I really wanted to, but Pat, Cathy, and Jeff did. So I figured I would too.

I started in the first grade I think. At first I loved it. But the music was sooooo boring. Of course, when you can only play one finger at a time, the music can't be particularly exciting. After a while, I dreaded it. I kinda gave up. But I didn't want to disappoint Mom, so I kept going. But as I got older, it became obvious I wasn't into it.

My teacher, Mrs. Andrews, was very old and a widow. Whether she was really very old, I have no idea. When you're six, anyone over thirty seems old. She started me in one piano lesson book series, but I couldn't handle it. She switched me to an easier series, but I still didn't practice much. I swear I was in the *Schaum B Book* for a million years.

But I kept going. Why? To this day, I'm not sure. But I struggled through. Sometimes she'd ask, "Now what lesson are we on?" and I'd skip a song I couldn't handle. I'm guessing she knew I was cheating, but she never said anything.

It went that way for years. But then one day, she said something that changed my life. She said, "I know you struggle with reading music. I'm going to teach you how to play by chords. I'm a little hesitant, because recently I showed another of my students, and he learned it very well. But he forgot almost completely how to read music."

Well, she did show me how to play chords. It really isn't an exaggeration to say it changed my life. While I never did get very good as a kid, in my young adult life, I went back to the piano and started to play songs by chords. Sometimes I'd find the chords written out, and sometimes I figured them out myself, which is basically playing by ear.

The sad thing is that Mrs. Andrews was right. I can't read music very well anymore.

But the good thing is, because of those few lessons in chords, I have had a pretty busy life playing piano. I've played in rock bands, praise bands, and folk trios. I sometimes play piano accompaniment at church, and I still routinely play and sing at small gatherings where they want some light entertainment. Recently, we "got the band back together," and our rock band is playing venues again. Music has become a huge part of my life. I'm not great, or immensely talented, but good enough to enjoy it. Which is enough for me.

If Mrs. Andrews hadn't taught me those last few lessons, none of it would have happened. I often wonder if I would've figured it out on my own. My gut feeling is that I wouldn't have. I'm incredibly grateful to her. Without her last bit of teaching, music would probably not be a big part of my life.

And I would be much poorer for it.

California

We're Going to Disneyland

Sometime in early 1962, when I was six, Mom and Dad made a big announcement to us. They said, "We are going to Disneyland!" To a six-year old, would anything have sounded better? Well, not much. We were, obviously, pretty excited.

But there was one problem. Disneyland is in California, almost 2,500 miles away. And in the 60s, normal families couldn't afford to fly cross-country. So we were going to drive. This was going to be *some* vacation. Honestly, it's still the most ambitious vacation I've ever been on.

Of course, we weren't driving all that way just for Disneyland. While Disneyland was the hook to get us kids on board, Mom and Dad really wanted to see their friends May and John, who had moved to Riverside, California, a few years earlier. We'd stay with them and hang out with their kids, Beth and Bob. But that was cool. We liked Beth and Bob. Of course, Disney World, in Florida, would be much closer. Except that Disney World wasn't a thing back in 1962.

You know what else wasn't a thing in 1962? Interstate highways. The entire National Highway System was approved by Congress in 1956, but by 1962, it wasn't anywhere near completion. Which means most of the roads we took were two-lane 60 MPH roads, with towns, stop signs, traffic lights, and all that goes with it. There were no bypasses back then, or at least not many. This was a different trip compared to what it would be today.

This was going to be a looooong trip. Honestly, I can't imagine a trip like this. It took five days of driving each way, so we'd be gone almost three weeks. And remember, in 1962, cars didn't have air conditioning. They didn't have seat belts. No cruise control. There was almost no fast food. And almost no chain hotels. No tablets, DVD players, or computers to play on. In other words, when driving each way, we had over five days straight of ten-hour days. And Dad drove every single mile. Our goal was 500 miles each day. In today's world, with cars being as comfortable as they are, and with speed limits of 70 to 75 MPH, 500 miles isn't that much. But back then, it was pretty brutal.

Even though it would be a lot of driving, Mom and Dad got us excited about it. (Pretty sure they kinda glossed over the 5,000 miles and ten-days-in-the-car part.) The trip was only possible because Dad had just received something I'd never heard of: a credit card. I wasn't sure exactly what that was, but I remember it was a Phillips 66 card. As Dad described it, "Phillips sent me this card to help me out, and asked me if I would use their gas." (I'm not sure that's exactly how it happened, but that's how he explained it.) Our job, as kids, was to keep our eyes out for Phillips 66 gas stations.

Early one morning, we loaded all our stuff, and ourselves, into the Buick for the long, long trip. Dad was in the driver's seat. Mom was in the passenger seat. Jeff, eight at the time, sat between them. Cathy, eleven, sat by the back left window. Pat, twelve, sat by the back right window. And me, at age six, sat in the back seat in the middle. On the hump. For the entire trip.

It's probably good I didn't understand how long we'd be in that car. I might have died.

This Land Is Your Land

On long trips today, how do you keep kids occupied? There are, of course, a whole bunch of ways, most dealing with some kind of tech or electronics. Those didn't exist in 1962, so Mom had to get creative.

We'd watch the scenery of course. But being the littlest and sitting on the hump, I couldn't see much. And scenery gets pretty boring, especially to a kid. So we had games.

We had to find letters on signs in ABC order. And the letters had to *start* the word. Otherwise it would be too easy. Actually, it was kind of a dumb game, because we all saw the same signs. Also, it was easy to cheat. ("I saw that letter, I really, really did!") Even if you got ahead, everyone else probably caught up when you were on X. Not a lot of words start with X.

Mom had a box of games as well. There were checkers games made for the car. There were books with word puzzles and things like that. There were books to read. And on and on. But still, ten hours a day is a long time for kids to entertain themselves.

When things got particularly bad, invariably Mom would say, "Let's sing." So we sang. As I've said, we were a musical family. I'm sure we sang a bunch of songs. For instance, we sang the world's most annoying song, "Ninety-nine Bottles of Beer on the Wall." I'm sure *that* didn't get old! The one I remember most was "This Land Is Your Land." I think we only knew the first verse, but we sang it over and over and over. I swear we sang it all the way to California. Okay, I'm sure we didn't, but it sure seemed like it.

I have to give my dad a little credit here. He was never a patient man. While he loved his kids, he wasn't one to hang out with us a lot, or to play games often. For him to sit in the car with all of us kids probably whining and complaining was pretty amazing. I honestly don't know if I could have done it.

Remember that our job was to look out for Phillips 66 stations? *Okay*, I thought, *I can do that*. I'm pretty sure Dad soon regretted giving us that job. Every single time I saw a Phillips 66, I had to yell, "There's a Phillips 66 station, Dad! Are we going to stop?" or some similar interjection. I didn't understand about gasoline and gas tanks, so I didn't realize you didn't have to stop at *every* single one. I'm sure Dad explained it to me, but I'm also pretty sure I still let him know each time I saw one.

But I never forgot my job. Every time I saw the red Phillips 66 sign, I made sure I told him. Every. Single. Time.

I'm sure Dad was having a great time.

Colorado Springs

We passed through Colorado Springs on this trip. It's memorable to me for three things. Now, just because I as a six-year-old found them memorable doesn't mean a whole lot. But they were interesting to me, at least at the time.

The first was that we saw the Air Force Academy. I never understood why we wanted to go there. All I know is that we did. And we went, and—it was closed.

How could an entire military academy be closed? For sixty years, I've wondered that. I'm pretty sure we wanted to see the chapel. I remember walking up to a very weird building and peering through the front doors. I'm sure it was the chapel. All I know is that we didn't see it, and Dad was disappointed. Me, why would I want to see some building? I didn't really care.

The second thing about that visit was irrigation ditches. As I remember it, some of the streets had tiny ditches next to them. Whether she was right or not, Mom told us they were irrigation ditches. Looking back on it, although I know Colorado has a lot of irrigation, I'm not sure they ran along city streets. Whatever they were, there were little water runways in front of where we were staying. I remember jumping across one. Unfortunately, just as I did, my watch fell off. Into the ditch it went.

I was really upset. I mean, it was my watch! I had felt very adult by having a watch. And now it was gone. So of course I ran into the house yelling, and everyone came out. We all looked, but with no luck. Even if we had found it, I doubt that a cheap 1962 watch would have been waterproof. Yes, I was bummed. But there was nothing to be done. So the big six-year old sucked it up. It was the only thing I could do.

My biggest memory from Colorado Springs was where we stayed. It wasn't a motel. It was more of a small house. We had the bottom floor, complete with bedrooms, a kitchen, and a living room.

When we got to that house and had all our luggage inside, we were going to swim at the pool. I remember distinctly what Mom told us as we were about to change into our swimsuits. She said, "You girls go change in the front bedroom, you boys change in the back bedroom, and Dad and I will change in the other one." No big deal, right? But my six-year-old brain picked up on something. She'd said "Dad and I will change." Really? They would change in the same room? But, but…Dad was a boy and Mom was a girl. Every little boy was taught that you're not supposed to try to see girls naked! That's what I was told, anyway. I didn't know that, apparently, there was an exception to this rule for married people. I told Mom, "You and Dad are going to change in the same room? I can't wait till I'm old and married and get to see my wife with no clothes on!"

I mean, Mom and Dad shared a bedroom and a bed. Did I really think the "Don't peek at naked girls" rule applied to married people? Apparently I did. I obviously had not thought it through. I do know it gave me an entirely different idea of what being married meant.

Nudity was included. Who knew!

Random Stops

Cathy, Jeff, Dick, Pat, and Mom at the Grand Canyon

This trip was really something. We went everywhere!

I remember going to the Petrified National Forest. Mostly I remember seeing a petrified lady. (Somehow I doubt that's true, but that's what I remember.) Jeff and I each got a piece of petrified wood as souvenirs. I wish I still had mine!

And of course we went to the Grand Canyon. I remember nothing, except Mom getting scared because Cathy was getting way too close to the rim. Cathy always lived a little on the edge, so it wasn't a real surprise. But Mom was convinced Cathy would fall. Luckily, she didn't.

We went to Mesa Verde, which basically are ancient Native American homes carved into rocks. It was impressive. We got to climb all around them. That was kinda cool, even for a kid.

My most vivid memory wasn't a stop at all. It was while we were traveling. We took a different route coming back than going out so we could stop at as many places as possible.

I don't know what route we took on the way back, but I remember it was hot. Dad said, "We're going to go through the desert." Well, we thought that would be really cool. We all had watched westerns, and we figured it would be just like them. I expected to see cattle skulls all over, because they were common in the movies. Alas, no cattle skulls.

I wanted to see tumbleweeds blowing all over. I thought we'd see gigantic herds of buffalo, or bison. I don't think we saw either; I think I'd remember that. Soon, it got boring.

Until the one thing we all knew about the desert hit us hard: the heat. Remember, there was no AC in this car. And we were packed in pretty tightly, so we were sticking to each other. As we drove, it got hotter. Kids are pretty resilient, but there's a limit.

Luckily, Dad had apparently planned for this. He had a big glass jug (plastic was not common in 1962) that he kept in the trunk. (How it fit with all our other stuff, I have no clue.) We stopped every half hour or so, and Dad opened the trunk, got the bottle out, and soaked a bunch of towels. We put those wet towels in the windows, on our shoulders, on our laps, everywhere we could. It cooled us for a while. But when the water evaporated, Dad had to stop, and we'd do it all over again.

I really thought I was going to die from the heat. (I sometimes leaned to the dramatic, I guess.) But I didn't die. We made it through. But it took a long time, and it was miserable.

I sometimes look back on that and wonder what Mom and Dad were thinking. Why would they do that to us? But I also remember that 1962 was different from the present day. They weren't being abusive, although it felt like it to me. They were doing the best they could. Most cars didn't have AC, and ours definitely didn't. We didn't have enough money to fly. And the West has lots of deserts. If we were going to Disneyland, we didn't have much choice but to drive through one of them.

So no, they weren't abusive. They were doing the best they could.

A Trip to the Moon

I don't remember much about Disneyland itself. But I do remember two things.

The first was the Matterhorn, a roller coaster. Actually, I remember *not* going on the Matterhorn. Most of my family did, I think. But I didn't. Maybe it was because I was too little and they wouldn't let me on. More likely I was being a chicken. I remember Mom asking me about it, and deciding I'd go on the Highway Cars, while the rest of them went on the roller coaster. Mom, of course, stayed with me. Even though I'm sure she'd have rather gone on the Matterhorn.

The cars were fun. All I did was sit there and pretend to steer. I had the car all to myself, with Mom waiting at the end. I felt so cool. It was on a track of course, so I couldn't mess up. All in all, it was a pretty tame ride, but fitting, probably, for a kid just out of first grade. At the very end of the ride, my car was heading toward a garage, and the doors were closed. As I got closer, I expected them to open, but they didn't. I kept getting closer, and I started to get really scared. Finally, at the last minute, they opened. It wasn't a glitch; it was supposed to be like that. I think I was just being a scaredy-cat.

My most distinct memory was the Rocket to the Moon. There was a very tall (to me) rocket, and we all went in and took a seat. A big movie screen showed what was happening.

I'm sure it was pretty tame. After all, it was 1962, and we didn't have 3D and CGI like we do now. If they had that ride today, I'm sure it would have looked, and probably felt, very realistic. But in 1962, we just sat in chairs and watched a video of us going to the moon and back. Still, I thought it was really cool. I always liked rockets and space, so it was great.

When it was over, I remember walking out and talking to my family about it. Now, remember how I've said I was a bright kid? Well, sometimes yes. But this time, not so much. I honestly thought we had traveled to the moon.

I should have known better. I knew about NASA and Project Mercury. I had an idea of how far away the moon actually was. But somehow I didn't put it all together.

When we were talking, it became clear to my family that I really thought we had been to the moon. One of them, I think Pat, said "Do you think we went to the moon?"

When she said that, I finally got it. Luckily. I answered, "No, I know we didn't. I was just kidding." Or something like that. And I tried to act real cool about it.

But I think they saw through me. (I was never a very good liar.) To their credit, they didn't make fun of me or anything.

Thankfully!

Age 7 and 8

Rusty

Rusty

Rusty was our dog. As I've mentioned, we'd previously had a dog named Peaches, but I have no memory of him. (Her?) Rusty is the only dog from my childhood that I really knew.

Rusty was part cocker spaniel, but mostly a mutt. I have no idea where we got her from, but I know I was very young. One day soon after we adopted her, we were showing her off to the milkman (yes, we had a milkman). He asked what her name was, and we said we hadn't decided yet. Mr. Paine, the milkman, took one look at this reddish dog and said, "Rusty. Why don't you name her Rusty?" So we did.

We took her to the veterinarian when we first got her, and we had the vet cut off Rusty's tail. Really! Is that still a thing? We were told it was commonly done to dogs so they wouldn't chase their tails. But Rusty used to chase her tail-stump anyway. Looking back, it seems cruel. But Rusty didn't complain, and honestly I think she accepted it pretty easily. Or at least that's what we believed.

As I've said, the 1960s was a good time to be a dog. There were no leash laws. When Rusty wanted out, we just opened the door and let her go. She always came back. While we obviously knew she was leaving piles all around the neighborhood, that was just what was done back then. If you happened to step in a pile of dog manure in your backyard, it was part of small- town living. We didn't complain to whoever we thought owned the dog. We just dealt with it.

Yes, letting a dog run posed some risks. She could have run away. She could have been hit by a car. She could have been stolen. But none of those things happened. Rusty had the run of the neighborhood, along with Queenie, Davey's dog, and Nipper, Johnny's dog.

Seeing a dog run alone today probably sends a whole bunch of people to social media reporting a lost dog. But in the 1960s, this was normal.

Being responsible pet owners, we had her "fixed." That was the term we used. We didn't say "spayed" or "neutered." No, Rusty was "fixed."

But one time, one of us kids said Rusty was an "it" because she had been fixed. Mom got pretty mad about that. I didn't know why until years later. Looking back, it makes sense. Earlier, Mom had had cervical cancer. She caught it early, had a total hysterectomy, and made a complete recovery. She said later she felt a sort of kinship with Rusty, because Mom had been "fixed" as well. She said, "I'm not an *it,* and neither is Rusty."

Fair enough.

To say I did everything with Rusty would be an exaggeration. But Rusty and I hung out a lot. She used to come with me on my paper route all the time. It was great. I feel bad for kids who grow up without a dog.

We all know how this story ends. All of us kids grew up. While Rusty was still our dog, we didn't spend all our time playing with her as we had when we were younger. And she aged. She started getting growths on her skin and slowing down. She had trouble walking. She had trouble controlling her bladder, and she started vomiting a lot. Eventually, my parents had to make the decision. The one all pet owners dread. The one where "It's time."

One Saturday morning, Mom and I took Rusty to the vet for the very last time. Rusty was so excited, because she always liked going to the vet. Mom and I struggled all the way there, seeing how Rusty was happier than she had been for a long time. But we knew we didn't have much choice. Rusty was no longer healthy, or really very happy.

We didn't take more than one step into that office, and all the people working there knew why we were there. I'm sure it was written all over our faces. The receptionist said simply, "Oh, you've done so much for her." And Rusty had no idea. She was still happy. But we went back with her and waited with her, till it was all over. And then we took her home and buried her.

I've only had two dogs in my life. Rusty, when I was a kid, and Pepper, in my adulthood. Somehow, all these years later, I still miss them both.

Over my lifetime, I've had multiple pets, and many of them we had to "put down." It's always so sad. But I know one thing: when I go, I want to go just like those pets did. In every case, they were surrounded by their entire family of loved ones. An IV was hooked up, some blue fluid went in, and…it was over.

I can't think of a better way to go.

Mail

When I was very little, I was always a bit fascinated by the mail. To me, it was somewhat magical. I mean, this guy walked up to our door and put letters in the box. Then Mom would get them, open them, and complain about some. Junk mail, bills, and other things comprised the bulk of our mail apparently.

But I thought it was cool that stuff could just show up at the door. Almost like magic.

The mail was *never* for me. I mean, never. You'd think I would have received some birthday cards at least. I probably did, but even so, that's just once a year. To a kid, that's like never. So one day I told Mom, "I wish I would get some mail."

She said something about how someone would have to write me a letter. I asked her how that worked exactly, and she explained about letters, stamps, and the Post Office. Once I understood that, I figured out how I could get some mail: I was going to write myself a letter.

It wasn't a long letter, maybe one or two pages. But it was handwritten, addressed to me, and signed by me. I have no idea what I told myself. Mom gave me a stamp, and then she showed me how to address it, put the stamp on, and put it in the mailbox.

MAIL

The next day I waited for the mailman. Well, he came, but there was no letter. No big deal; I could wait. And I did. It wasn't too long before, lo and behold, there was a letter for me. From me.

I know it seems really stupid, but I was pretty excited. I actually had some mail. Yay! I ripped it open and read it straight through. Of course, since I had written it, there were no surprises. While it was kinda fun, I realized it wasn't the same as getting real mail. Still, I thought it was better than nothing.

Mom? She just looked at me and laughed. She wasn't laughing at me. I think she was laughing because she realized her youngest child was a little different, but not in a bad way. At least, that's what I imagine she was thinking. She might have been thinking *What an idiot*, but I doubt it. That wasn't how Mom worked.

You can imagine how excited I was when I got real mail. When I was older and ordered rockets by mail order and they showed up, that was a huge day. Any mail was a big deal.

Of course, many decades later, two things are now clear. First, the mailbox of my childhood was tiny by today's standards, about the size of a hardcover book. I have no idea how all the mail fit in. I'm guessing we didn't get as much junk mail back then, but I don't know. The other thing: I understand Mom's grumbling. Because that's what I do now with the mail, just like she did. "Junk mail and bills." I know now why she didn't get excited about the mail like I did.

Some things are just more exciting to kids!

Gravity

Yes, gravity.

One day I was walking up the stairs to the bedrooms. I was holding a ball, and I dropped it. Of course, it fell down. It bounced on just about every step before it finally fell into the kitchen at the bottom of the steps.

I remember asking myself, *Why did it go down?* I mean, more generally, why does everything fall down? What is special about down? Why don't things fall up?

I, of course, had no idea. I was only about seven. I didn't know any physics. I had never heard of Isaac Newton. And the concept of gravity was unknown to me.

Years later, having been a physics teacher, I could have explained to my younger self about the attraction all things in the universe have for each other, called gravity.

But I didn't know any of those things. I just knew everything fell *down*. Therefore, there must be something special about *down*.

I stayed on the stairs for quite a while, dropping the ball, then throwing it up, then throwing it across, etc. No matter what I did, it always fell down. Never up. That didn't give me any answers, but it did confirm there was something special about *down*.

GRAVITY

I'm pretty sure I wasn't the first little kid to wonder about that. All I know is that I didn't have any answers. I'm also sure that if I had asked Mom or Dad, or even my older sisters, they probably could have explained it to me. But apparently I didn't think it was really all that important, because I don't think I ever asked anyone. I just kept wondering.

It would be a much cooler story if I had actually delved into it more. I mean, discovering the concept of gravity at seven years old would be pretty neat. But apparently I wasn't that cool. Or that smart.

I just wondered, then moved on. Alas.

The Chocolate Bunny

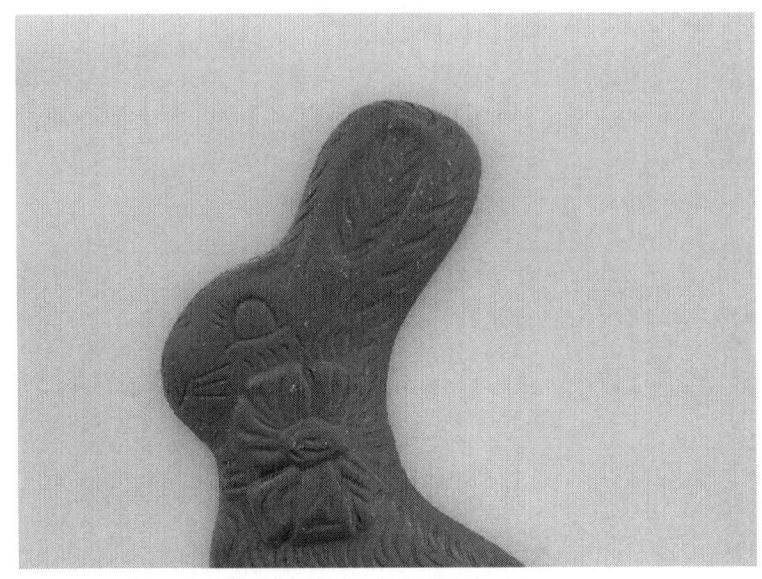

Chocolate bunny, similar to one I gave Mom

    I know I'm constantly saying how different life was when I was a kid, but every time I write about it, it hits me all over again.

    For instance, right around the corner from our house, in a completely residential area, was a chocolate shop. Really. The Quisnos lived on Fifth Street, in a normal house like the rest of us. But Mrs. Quisno had a chocolate shop in her basement. She had an outside stairway off her driveway that led down to the store. I'm guessing she didn't have it inspected; the health department probably didn't even know about it. But she sold chocolate. I doubt something like that could happen today.

Looking back on it, I'm sure she didn't make her own chocolate, even though we assumed she did. I'm guessing she bought chocolate in bulk and poured it into her molds. But that didn't matter, because we were convinced that Quisno's chocolate was the best! And honestly, to this day, I still liked her white chocolate better than any I've had since. Probably nostalgia, but that's how I remember it.

This wasn't a place we went to get a candy bar. But it *was* a place we'd go for special occasions. One year, just before Easter, I went to Quisno's to pick out some Easter candy for Mom. I got a huge solid chocolate bunny. As I remember it, the bunny was at least a foot tall. And maybe it was. But time has a funny ability to make everything in our childhood seem bigger than it actually was. So maybe it was only eight inches. But still, it was big. And I was *so* proud to have bought this, all by myself, with my own money, for Mom. I have no idea where I got the money, but somehow I had it.

When Easter came, I gave it to her, and she was so grateful. She thanked me up and down, and said all the things I wanted to hear. I was proud. Mom was happy. All was well.

Until it wasn't. A few weeks later (I don't remember the occasion or the reason), we were on the back porch going through a box of stuff to throw out. While we were going through the stuff that was, essentially, trash, I came across that bunny! It was still in its wrapper, not a bite taken out of it. It was clear that Mom was throwing away my gift. The gift I was so proud of. There it was. In the trash.

I remember this exactly. I remember where I was standing, where the box of trash was, and where Mom was sitting. When I saw the bunny, I looked at Mom with such dejection. How could she throw my precious present away?

When she saw it, and saw that I saw it, she immediately felt horrible. She knew exactly how I felt. She tried to explain that she was "on a diet" and although she really appreciated the gift, she just couldn't eat it, on her diet.

I understood that, on some level, but still I was crushed. And she felt so bad. She knew she had hurt me, and Mom never wanted to be the cause of her kids' pain. No mom does. But this time, she was.

Well, of course I got over it. Or maybe I didn't. I mean, sixty years later I still remember it. So maybe it stuck with me a little more than I like to admit.

The odd thing about it was, Mom wasn't stupid. Why didn't she take it right out to the garbage can? Or take it to work and leave it in the break room? Or…anything except throw it in the trash. I've never been able to figure that out. I do know, though, that she never expected me to see that.

Did it scar me? No. Did it hurt me at the time? Yes. Did Mom regret it? 100 percent. I know she would have given anything to not let me see that. But I did.

As adults, we often don't completely realize how little kids think, no matter how hard we try. We forget how easily they get their feelings hurt. We forget how sometimes they try so hard to please us. And when we forget those things, sometimes we hurt them even when we try not to.

Many years later, my child, Emma, got me a pair of gym shorts for Christmas. They had the cartoon Tasmanian Devil on them. She was so proud, because I really liked them. Unfortunately, they were way too small. I couldn't even fit in them. So I had no choice but to exchange them. Well, they had Taz shorts, but they weren't exactly the same. When Emma saw them, she cried and cried. I'm sure she felt exactly like I did when I saw that bunny. I had hurt her just like Mom had hurt me. And like Mom, I felt horrible.

Luckily though, most kids are resilient. They get over things. As I did. (And Emma did.) I didn't hold it against Mom. I'm sure by the next day all was well.

But boy, at the time, it really hurt. Both of us.

Milky Way

In third grade, I walked home from school every day for lunch. Well, most days anyway. But this day must have been special, because after lunch I walked back to school eating a Milky Way. Not a fun-size one, but a real, full-size candy bar. It wasn't common that we got candy bars for no special occasion, so this was rare. But as I was walking to school, I must have had enough. Or maybe I wanted to save it for later. Or something. All I know is that I put the Milky Way in my pocket. And completely forgot about it.

Well, until a few days later, when I heard Mom in the laundry room, calling my name.

I went out there, and she was holding up my pants, with a very questioning look on her face. They had just come out of the dryer, and there was a problem. Apparently, I'd never finished that Milky Way. Forgot about it completely. And those pants, complete with the candy bar, went through the washer and the dryer.

Okay, that's really odd. Not that I forgot about it. As a kid, I was always forgetting things. That was part of who I was. What was odd was that Mom didn't find it. She *always* checked pockets before washing stuff. But somehow she missed this one.

MILKY WAY

The result was that the pocket was essentially glued shut. I have no idea if there was chocolate all over the washer and dryer, but I don't know how there could *not* have been. All I know is that Mom was holding the pants up with a *what is the meaning of this* expression.

I don't think I got in real trouble for it. Mom knew it wasn't intentional. So while she was not pleased, I hadn't meant to do it, so I think I got off pretty light.

Honestly, that may have been the last time I didn't finish a candy bar. Probably because I love chocolate. But maybe, somewhere in the back of my mind, is my eight-year-old self is saying, "Don't put it away; you'll forget about it."

You never know.

July 20, 1963

When I started writing this, I didn't remember the date exactly. I had to research it a bit. Now that I have, I know July 20 is the correct date. What happened on that date? Well, I was seven years old, and it was the first time in my life, at least that I can remember, when I had a really, really big decision to make. For most of my life, I've wondered if I made the right choice. But now, sixty years later, in light of things, I think I did.

What was this momentous, life-changing, gut-wrenching decision? It may not seem like much now, but to a seven-year-old, it was huge. On that day, two separate events would happen. The first was that *The Sword in the Stone*, the Disney animated movie about King Arthur as a boy, was showing at the local theater. But also, a solar eclipse was going to happen. Not only the same day, but also the same time.

Why was that so hard?

Take yourself back to 1963. There were no multiplexes, at least in my small town. No, there was only one (very large) theater. And they didn't show movies over and over. I mean, they did sometimes, but Disney movies were different. My memory, which might be wrong, was that most movies cost a dime, but Disney movies were twenty-five cents. And I think they only had one showing. Well, at least they only had one showing I was allowed to attend. So if I didn't see that movie showing on that Saturday afternoon, I wouldn't get to see it. Remember, there was no "Wait till it comes out on video" or "We'll catch it on Disney Plus." I assume it was playing in other towns at different times, but that wasn't an option. If I missed this showing, I missed it completely. The next time I'd be able to see that movie was when it was on *Walt Disney's Wonderful World of Color*, a TV show that ran on Sunday nights. But that wouldn't happen for a few years. To a seven-year-old, "a few years" might as well be a lifetime.

On the other hand: the eclipse. I was kind of an astronomy nerd as a kid, and the idea of the eclipse really fascinated me. I had read about how the light changes, the sounds change, animals sometimes do weird things, and all of that. And it really intrigued me. I really, really wanted to see it.

But there was the movie. I had to make a choice. Which?

I chose the movie. And it killed me. (Okay, not literally. I'm here writing this.) The movie was great, and I was glad I'd seen it. I remember walking home, looking up and seeing a tiny bit of what was left of the eclipse. It wasn't anything like I had read about, but again, it was the tail end.

All my life, I kinda sorta somewhat regretted that decision. Looking back on it, movies came all the time. Eclipses are exceedingly rare. But it wasn't until recently that I finally forgave my seven-year-old self and let me believe my decision was the right one.

Why? Because I recently looked up that eclipse. In my hometown, it wasn't total at all. It was a partial eclipse. Which means it would have been pretty cool, but not nearly as cool as a total eclipse. I know that firsthand because in 2017, fifty-four years after that decision, I *did* see a solar eclipse. There was one down south, and we drove about ten hours to see the few minutes of totality. And it did not disappoint. However, the only really cool part was during totality, which didn't happen in 1963. If I had skipped the movie, I would have been disappointed.

There was another reason I made the right call. I really liked that movie. The story of Arthur really resonated with me. It wasn't until many years later, as an adult, I read the book the movie was based on: *The Once and Future King*, by T.H. White. The book was wonderful, engaging, entertaining, and incredibly thought-provoking. I won't say that book changed my life, but it did have a big influence on me. If I had never seen the movie, I probably wouldn't have read the book. So there's that.

It was really tough making that decision. Neither of my parents made it for me. I had to choose for myself. Yes, at the time I regretted it. But it taught me something: sometimes we have to choose between two things we really desire. We have to pick one. And then live with the consequences of that choice. And that was what I did. I'll give my seven-year-old self some props, because, as far as I remember, I didn't whine, cry, or complain. I made the choice and accepted it. For better or for worse.

And that's all we can ask of a kid. Or an adult.

JFK

The year was 1960. I had just turned five. Mom came to me and said, "Sit and watch this. Someday you'll be able to talk about it."

Okay, maybe those weren't her exact words, but close enough. And I don't think it was just me. I'm pretty sure my brother Jeff was with me.

What did Mom want us to watch? The Nixon-Kennedy debate. Or one of them at least.

Now, why would Mom think a five-year old kid would care about a presidential debate? My guess is that this was the 1960 equivalent of putting on a video for your child, or giving him a tablet to play on. I don't know. But I know one thing: she was right. I do remember it, and I can talk about it. Why I remember it, I have no idea. I saw two men talking, in black and white of course. And it was real boring. But I stayed and watched it, because I was supposed to. I'm sure I had no idea what they were talking about.

But yes, I remember the Nixon-Kennedy debate.

That's not my last memory of JFK. Of course not. If you're anywhere near my age, you know what I'm getting at.

My next JFK memory is a few years later, when I was in third grade. School had just let out, and I was walking across the playground, getting ready to walk home. One of the big kids, a fifth-grader, yelled to me, "President Kennedy was shot!"

I knew that couldn't be right. Those things just don't happen. So I walked home. About ten minutes later I walked in the back door and said "Mom, I'm home." As I walked into the living room, I saw her. She had pulled a chair right up to the TV. She was watching it, and crying. I'll never forget that.

The big kid was right. Because the President had been assassinated in the afternoon, our teachers didn't know about it. Or maybe they just didn't tell us; I'm not sure. But now I knew that fifth-grader was right.

Mom sat watching, and she couldn't stop crying. I didn't know it then, but when I got older and started to understand politics and government, I found out Mom was a pretty staunch Republican. I'm sure she didn't vote for JFK. Yet, he was the president, and he had been killed. And Mom cried.

That image has stuck with me for the last sixty years: Mom crying in front of the TV. So many of my memories show how different the world was during my childhood, and this is one more example. Mom was a Republican, didn't vote for JFK, but she still was completely distraught when he was killed.

It was a sad day for America. Mom knew that, even if she hadn't voted for him.

I'm not sure so many of us today would react the same way to an assassination of someone we hadn't voted for. Like I said, the world was different then.

For better or for worse.

My Early Bikes

Dick with his new bike

    Bikes really are an essential part of a kid's growing up. It's one of my few childhood items that still seem important to kids today. They give kids freedom, speed, and just plain fun.

    Before a kid gets a bike, he usually has a tricycle. We had two. There was a red one, pretty much like every other kid's trike. It was little and easy to pedal. Great for a beginner. But we also had a gigantic green chain-driven tricycle. It fit two. I remember riding around on this thing with Jeff pedaling and me standing on a support on the back. It was great. I've never seen another like it.

Eventually, most kids graduate to a two-wheeler. Because most kids learn to ride around the age of five or six, it has to be a little bike. Today, I think most kids get a new bike of their own when they hit that age. That makes a lot of sense. But back then, that's not how it usually worked. Nobody had that kind of money.

When my oldest sister, Pat, learned how to ride a bike, we bought a little green twenty-inch bike from some friends. Actually, that's not true. We didn't buy it; Pat did. For eight dollars. Yep, she bought a used bike for the grand total of eight dollars. Where Pat came up with eight dollars, I have no idea. But that was the deal.

It worked out pretty well. Because while us four kids were close in age, we were far enough apart that by the time a younger kid could ride a bike, the older kid had grown out of it. So when Cathy learned how to ride a bike, she bought the little green bike from Pat. For six dollars. (I guess because it was now a little more used.) When Jeff needed a bike, Cathy sold him the little green bike for four dollars. Then I bought it from Jeff for two dollars. You can see where this is going. Since each kid essentially paid two dollars for the bike, I had to *give* it away. To make it even. Even as a little kid, I could see that was fair.

By about second grade, each of us was ready for a "big bike." When Jeff was in second grade, he asked for a bike for Christmas. On Christmas morning, we wanted to run downstairs and open all our presents. Like every little kid everywhere since the beginning of Christmas, I think. But that year,

Pat and Cathy said we had to "wait just a bit." Finally, we were allowed to come down. We ran downstairs, and right in front of the tree, complete with a big bow, was Jeff's new bike. It was a bright red Murray, a full twenty-six-inch big kid's bike. It was pretty exciting. As soon as the rest of the presents were opened, he took it out to ride it. (In the snow of course.) And he loved it.

A year later, on Christmas again, we wanted to run downstairs, but again we were told to wait just a bit. Okay, I wasn't stupid. I'm a year younger than Jeff, so I thought I knew what was happening. I wanted to run downstairs so fast, but Pat and Cathy wouldn't let me. There was nothing to do but wait. Sure enough, when we finally ran downstairs, there was *my* new bike. No, I wasn't really surprised, but it didn't matter; I still was excited. It was a black and red AMF Roadmaster, and it was perfect. I too took it out for a test ride. Also in the snow.

I had that bike for about five years, and it served me well. I rode it everywhere, and when I got my paper route, it was indispensable. But to be honest, I'm still a little mad at my friend Jay. Because I let Jay ride my *new* bike, and he fell on it and broke the front light. I was so upset, but there was nothing to be done. The light was bent, plain and simple. Sixty years later, maybe I should forgive Jay? You think?

I felt like that bike was my ticket to freedom, because I could ride all over town, which I did. That bike really set me free. It was my steed playing around the neighborhood. It was my transportation when we took bike hikes. Which we did often, on the spur of the moment, without telling a parent about it. As long as we were home for supper, all was well. It was great.

I assume kids today still love their bikes. Whether it's still a ticket to freedom, I have no idea. For my own kids, in the late 90s, it was just as important to them as it was to me. For kids today, I don't know. It's a different world, and kids don't have quite the independence we had, I don't think. But for me, the bike was everything. I was so grateful.

Although I'm still a little mad at Jay!

The Cottage

Jeff and Dick catching a fish at the cottage

Uncle Bill was my mom's younger brother. He lived with Grandma and Grandpa, but he owned a small cottage near Fremont on the Sandusky River, just about a fifteen-minute drive from our house. This wasn't our cottage, so we didn't go there all the time. But we went there a lot, whenever Bill and Grandma and Grandpa were there.

Calling this a cottage is a bit of an exaggeration. First of all, it was tiny. It had a porch facing the river, and behind that was a very tiny kitchen, along with another small room that served as a bedroom and a living room. Notice what it didn't have? A bathroom. Instead, there was an outhouse out back. Somehow, it didn't seem weird having to go to the outhouse. For a little kid, somehow it was kinda fun.

Sometimes we'd go there on a Sunday afternoon. Sometimes we'd go in the evening. But every year, without fail, we went to the Nitschke family reunion. That was Mom's side of the family. These were great. Not because I got to see my relatives. Honestly, the only ones I knew well were my cousins Jeri and Jon. They lived in Michigan and didn't come to Ohio all that often. But they always made it to the family reunions, so that was nice. We always had fun with Jeri and Jon.

During these reunions, there was *so much food*. We ate until we were stuffed. But what was really cool was Grandpa had a huge washtub for the cold drinks. My memory tells me it was about six feet across. But knowing how kids' memories exaggerate sizes, it was probably a standard washtub, maybe three feet across. Instead of ice cubes, he always had a big block of ice. They're hard to find now, but they're actually kinda cool. He'd cover all the drinks, and the block of ice, with a heavy blanket, and they'd stay cold all day. And it was filled with soda pop.

Coke? Pepsi? No, none of those. Instead, he had a zillion bottles of Cotton Club beverages. I don't think Cotton Club exists anymore, but I think it was a local bottling company back then. There seemed to be every flavor imaginable—grape, cherry, cola, strawberry, root beer, black raspberry…and we got to drink *as much as we wanted*. We didn't get much pop at home, so this was a real treat.

Uncle Bill had a boat docked there. We didn't go out in the boat all that much, but we fished from the dock all the time. We didn't usually catch much, but sometimes we did. Grandpa had what he called a "live box." It was basically a cage about three feet across. When he'd catch a fish, he'd put the fish in the box and lower it into the river. The fish would live quite a while, so he could cook it whenever he wanted.

One day, Jeff and I were fishing on the dock and not catching anything. We were pretty bummed. When Mom called us for supper, we left the poles on the dock, with the lines still in the water. We used to do that quite a bit, in the hope that when we came back a fish would be on our hooks. Well, that never happened.

To be more accurate, it had never happened before. Because when Jeff and I went back to the dock, we could tell we both had a fish on our lines. When we reeled it in, the fish was all tangled in both of our lines, and both hooks were in his mouth. We had jointly caught a fish. We were excited! And the fish was huge. We were so proud, and pleased.

This would be the end of the story. But years later, when I was much older, I was talking to Mom about those family reunions. Then she said, "Do you remember that big fish you and Jeff caught together?"

"Of course," I replied. "That was neat. It was amazing how it all happened, with that fish on both hooks."

"Well, it wasn't exactly like that," she said. "While you were eating, Grandpa went down to the dock, took a fish out of his live box, and hooked it to both of your hooks. He wrapped the lines all up to make it look like it got messed up naturally."

"Really? Grandpa did that?" Although it was years later, I felt a little hurt, thinking Grandpa had lied to us all this time. That feeling lasted for about a half second before I realized Grandpa did it out of love. And it had worked. Jeff and I were both so happy, and so proud.

"Yes, he did. He couldn't stand seeing you two so upset that you hadn't caught anything. You know, Grandpa Clarence was always like that. He didn't like seeing kids unhappy. So when we weren't catching anything, he figured he could fix that. And he did."

So our catch wasn't actually a catch at all. But we didn't know that. We just knew we had a fish on our line, and that made us very glad.

Thank you, Grandpa. That was pretty cool.

Soaky

Two houses down from us lived an older family with no young kids. However, they had grandkids. Whenever Chris and Greg came to visit their grandparents, we'd usually find them to go play. We always liked it when they were around; it seemed cool and fun to hang out with friends who weren't part of our normal group.

One hot summer day, Chris and Greg came to visit, and we went over and started playing. (Years later, I'm amazed kids could go meet someone and just play.) But this time, the kids in the next house over were out as well. The Fosters had four kids, but they were much younger than us, so they weren't in our normal group of friends. For some reason, they were out in their backyard, along with their dad. I knew who Mr. Foster was, but I didn't really know him. My sister Pat used to babysit for them all the time, but I had no knowledge of him, or even the kids. But this time was different.

Jeff and I, along with Chris and Greg, started a water fight. I think it started with squirt guns, pretty sure. It was tame, but we were having a great time. All of a sudden, Mr. Foster came over and started to talk to us. Which was odd, because we didn't know him at all. He wasn't exactly outgoing; he always seemed too proper to be out back playing with kids. He was an insurance salesman who always wore a suit, for whatever that's worth.

But this time, he joined in. (He wasn't wearing a suit!) He started squirting us back, but then he grabbed the garden hose. Before we knew it, it was all-out war. And we were having the best time. Jeff, me, Chris, Greg, and Mr. Foster. I think some of his older kids joined in as well. We were yelling at each other, charging like it was war, and running around like crazy. We must have had a couple hoses, because I remember we were squirting each other. Jeff found a garbage can lid (they were metal back then) and used it as a shield. But Mr. Foster was going nuts, charging, spraying, and screaming like a man possessed. All in good fun, of course. It didn't take long until we were all as wet as wet can be.

I remember calling him "Soaky" because he was as wet as we were. Soaky was a brand of bubble bath back then that came in very neat bottles. The bottles were pretty much toys, because they were Disney characters, or other cartoons. So when the bubble bath was empty, you still had a toy. Cool.

We were yelling and screaming, calling him "Soaky" and having so much fun we didn't want to stop. Eventually, though, it ran its course, and we all went home. We talked about that day for weeks. It had been so much fun.

The funny thing, though, is how that experience was a one-off. Nothing like that with Mr. Foster ever happened again. I remember seeing him a few days later. I grinned and waved, and yelled, "Hey, Soaky!"

He gave a polite wave. That was all. The "fun" Mr. Foster was gone and the "insurance salesman" Mr. Foster was back.

I was a little sad, honestly. One day, there was plain magical fun. But after that, the magic was gone, almost like it never happened.

I have no idea what caused "Insurance salesman Mr. Foster" to morph into "Soaky Mr. Foster" that day. It was so much fun that I never forgot it. If only we could have recreated that day.

But maybe it's better it was a one-off. Because it made the memory a little more special.

An addendum: Whenever I think of "Soaky," I can't help singing the jingle in my head. These words aren't exact, but it goes something like this:

Soaky soaks you clean in oceans full of fun.
Scrubbly bubbly flibbly flubbly, clean before you're done.
Soaky soaks you clean, and every girl and boy Gets a toy when it's empty;
when it's empty it's a toy.

Swimming Lessons

City Beach in Port Clinton, where swimming lessons were held

A cork. That's where I started. A "cork" was the beginner level in swimming lessons. I can't remember if we started at cork, or if we had to demonstrate we could hold our breath or something. But if I remember right, we were given a cork on a string to wear around our neck.

Yes, swimming lessons: something to look forward to in the summer. This was before pools were common. The city had one (it's since been filled in to make a flower garden), but it was small, not nearly big enough for the multitudes of kids in swimming lessons.

So we learned to swim in Lake Erie, at City Beach.

I really have no idea how that worked. The beach in Port Clinton is very gradual. You have to walk way out in the water to get very deep. And of course there were waves; while they can be fun, they made it difficult to teach beginners. Also, it was June. Lake Erie in June is pretty cold. I remember getting so cold my lips turned blue. When that happened, some poor volunteer had to walk me back onto the beach so I could warm up.

"Cork" was the first classification. I think we had to float on our backs for a certain period of time to earn "guppy." After that, when we progressed more, we'd become "turtles."

We really, really wanted to advance. While we didn't get an award, what we got was better: a round patch to be sewn onto our swim trunks. That was pretty cool. I mean, a cork was fine and all, but when you could strut around with a turtle on your swimsuit, that was something.

I remember taking this patch home and giving it to Mom. She'd get out her sewing machine and sew it on. Apparently, that was just expected in the 60s. It was assumed we all had a Mom at home who had the time and ability to sew these patches on. Even though I know life was much different back then, that whole concept still throws me. What about the kids who didn't have moms? Or what if the mom couldn't sew? Or how about the Ritter family, who had ten kids? How many patches did Mrs. Ritter have to sew on? Or what about the (few) moms who worked full time? I have no idea. All I know is that I loved getting a new round white patch with a picture of a guppy or turtle on it.

The extreme, most coveted level was "fish." Honestly, I'm not sure I ever made that. I'm pretty sure the instructors would get about fifty feet apart or so, and the student had to swim back and forth between them, freestyle. Now, while Lake Erie really is a nice place to swim, it's not easy. Like I said before, it's uncommon for the lake to be calm; there's usually some waves on it, many times huge ones. I assume we canceled lessons if the water got too rough, but most days, there are some significant waves. We had to swim in it regardless. Also, while Lake Erie is much cleaner than most people realize, it's never particularly clear, especially near the shore where the sand is always kicked up, making the water somewhat murky. We didn't ever open our eyes underwater. While there were face masks for snorkeling, swim goggles hadn't been invented yet. Of if they did, none of us had them.

But all us kids went through swimming lessons. It made sense. Since we lived on a lake, and some parents had boats, it was useful to know how to swim, just in case.

However, Dad didn't really buy into all this. I remember him saying, "When I was a kid, my grandpa threw me in the river. I didn't know how to swim, but I learned pretty fast." I'm not convinced Dad was being 100 percent honest with this, but that's what he always said. I think he kinda thought swimming lessons weren't really needed. But he never threw any of us in the water to see if we could learn to swim on our own, but maybe that's because Mom might literally have killed him if he had!

SWIMMING LESSONS

In later years, when they built the new high school, it had a pool, and they used that from then on for swimming lessons. I was older then, so I missed that. While I think community swim lessons faded away for a while, I know they continue to offer them now. Which is a good thing.

While it makes a whole lot of sense to have the lessons in a pool, looking back on it, there was something special about having to swim in the lake to learn. All I know is that we really loved swimming lessons, we loved getting a new patch, and we felt pretty cool when we could actually swim.

Swimming lessons were one of the little joys of life.

Second Grade

Second grade started out rough. We had two elementary schools in town, and our house was kinda on the dividing line. In first grade, I went to Bataan Memorial Elementary. I was very comfortable there. But in second grade, I was switched to Jefferson Elementary. All the friends I had made in first grade were just…gone. I had to start all over.

The good part is that Mrs. Murphy, my teacher, was wonderful. She really cared for all of us and made us feel welcome and comfortable. That helped a lot. I soon got used to the new school, with new friends. Even though it was a little farther away, it was close enough I could still walk to school. I never, even through high school, had to take a bus.

What I remember most are the spell downs. Most of the country calls them spelling bees I think, but we had spell downs. We'd all stand up in a long line, and Mrs. Murphy would read words we had to spell. If we missed it, we had to sit down, and do some other work. Somehow, I almost never missed any words. In fact, I won almost every spell down. It got to the point, finally, that Mrs. Murphy wouldn't let me be in them. She said she wanted to give the other kids a chance. She found something else for me to do during them. You'd think I would've been upset. I mean, what kid doesn't like winning? But somehow I was okay with it. I think she gave me other fun

SECOND GRADE

things to do. So that was okay. After all, it was cool to be smart, so I couldn't complain too much.

One day, though, we were doing spelling dictation. She'd read us a sentence and we had to print it out. (Whenever she said "dictation," I looked up, because my name was Dick, and "dictation" kinda caught me.) I loved dictation, because I could spell anything. Or so I thought.

One day she read the sentence, "A little mouse sat on top of my sled." I quickly started printing it out. Until I got to the word *of.* Such a little word; it should have been easy. But apparently, I had never seen that word before. I knew the word of course, but I couldn't remember seeing it written. Neither had my classmates, because we all looked up in confusion, at about the same time.

Mrs. Murphy just smiled. I did what I always did: I sounded it out. Which means I wrote *of* as *uv.* That made sense. Unfortunately, of course, that's not correct. When it was all done and she showed us, the *o-f* spelling made complete sense. Not all words can be sounded out.

There came one other day when I found out I wasn't quite as smart as I thought. We were assigned a story to read, and one of the characters was named Pierre. Mrs. Murphy asked, "Does anyone know how to pronounce this name?"

Everybody started raising their hands, making guesses. They were all wrong. But I knew how to say it. After all, I was the best speller in the class. And in second grade, most words can be figured out by sounding them out. So when I saw

"Pierre," I sounded it out. I waited a while, then raised my hand. I knew I had it right. (Even if some of my classmates didn't get it.) When she called on me, I very confidently said, "Pie-REE." I knew that had to be correct.

But to my shock, she said, "No, that's not right either."

What? I couldn't be wrong! I was the best speller in the class. She *must* have heard me wrong. That had to be it. In my seven-year-old confidence, I raised my hand again. When she called on me again, I repeated, "Pie-REE."

Once again, she said, "No."

I couldn't believe it. I was wrong.

Finally, someone else guessed, "Pee-AIR," and she said, "That's right."

Huh. Who knew? Maybe I wasn't quite as smart as I thought. But to give myself a little credit, while I was surprised I was wrong, I wasn't mad about it. I remember thinking the girl who got it right must be pretty smart too. I can't remember, but I wonder if it was Jane. She was the second-best speller in the class, so maybe.

That wasn't the only time something like that happened. Another time, we were assigned the poem "As I Was Going to St. Ives." For some reason, I still remember it. It goes like this:

As I was going to St. Ives,
I met a man with seven wives.
Each wife had seven sacks,
Each sack had seven cats,

Each cat had seven kits
Kits, cats, sacks, wives,
How many were going to St. Ives?

She let us use paper and pencil to figure the answer. I remember feeling pretty cool when some kids were trying to do all the high-level arithmetic.

I knew the answer without doing any calculations. I knew it two ways: one, it was obvious, to me anyway, that there were seven of each, so I knew the answer was seven. (Yes, you've probably figured out I was wrong!) I also knew the answer another way. My brother was one grade ahead of me, and he had the same poem a year earlier. I remembered him saying the answer was seven. Okay, let's say I *thought* I remembered him saying that. Obviously, I was mistaken!

When she asked, "How many are going to St. Ives?" my hand shot up.

I proudly said, "Seven."

Once again, I was wrong. But this time I didn't say it twice. I'll give my seven-year-old self some credit for that anyway, because when someone came up with the right answer, I completely understood.

In case you haven't figured it out (spoiler alert), the answer, of course, is *one*. Since the narrator was going *to* St. Ives, the people he met must have been coming *from* St. Ives. And that made sense, so I was okay with my wrong answer.

The good news is, Mrs. Murphy still wouldn't let me in the spell downs. So I guess I was still smart!

A Very Bad Day
(But It Could Have Been Worse)

This happened one day when I was in early elementary school. I think it was third grade, but I can't be sure. I know I was very little.

I was walking home from school. We used to stick to the alleys rather than the streets, at least for the most part. Not only was it safer, but by the way everything was laid out, it was shorter. On this day, since I was taking the alley, I approached our house from the backyard. As I was walking toward the house, my brother ran to me screaming and waving his arms like a lunatic. I had no idea what he was saying. He was pretty incoherent, with panic in his voice.

As I got closer to the house, it became obvious. There, sitting on the ground, was my mom. She had a towel wrapped around her ankle, and the towel was soaked in blood. Yeah, something bad had happened.

Mom had been painting a wooden door. She'd propped it against the garage. She'd been using the kitchen stepladder to get to the top parts. In those days, stepladders were made of wood, and not always the sturdiest. This one was no exception. She'd unfolded the stepladder and was standing on one of the stop steps. The ladder was only about three feet tall, so you wouldn't think it was dangerous. But it wasn't on a level surface, and it shifted out from under her. As she fell, the ladder collapsed, and her right ankle got caught in it.

That was the exact moment Jeff got home from school.

Imagine you're Jeff. He's only one year older than me, so he was a little kid himself. He was the first to find Mom. She had *just* fallen. And it wasn't pretty. It was a compound fracture, so one of her leg bones was sticking out of her skin. It had to be hard on Jeff, finding Mom like that. He'd come home just a few minutes before me. And found her, on the ground, with her leg at some odd angle, with a protruding bone. Yeah, I can understand why he was upset.

There was no 911 in those days, so Mom told him to go next door and tell the neighbors, which he did. They were very helpful, and called the ambulance. Then she asked for a towel, which he got her, and she wrapped her ankle with it. That's when I walked onto the scene.

Shortly after, the ambulance arrived. They loaded her up, took her to the emergency room, and performed the required surgery.

She got through it, of course. But honestly, her leg was never the same. The ankle always did give her trouble. She could walk just fine, but she sometimes had a limp. Not always, but it was a problem. I'm pretty sure running would have been out of the question. But it didn't seriously affect her life after that, except some random pains and some limping.

Honestly, I'm glad Jeff found her. I don't know if I would have been as good as he was. He was understandably very upset, but through it all, he handled it very well. The odd thing about it, looking back, was that I wasn't really upset. Of course, I didn't see it. If I had seen her tibia poking out of her leg, I'm sure I'd have been as upset as Jeff. But I didn't, so I wasn't.

To this day, when I think of her, I often think of her right ankle. It never looked the same again, and it just kinda became part of her. But Mom, being Mom, never complained. She went about life, and work, as if it was all part of living.

Which it was. She made sure it was just part of living. And never complained. That was how Mom was.

How Fast Is 5 MPH?

The long road back to the cottage

As I've said, my grandparents (Clarence and Marvel) and my Uncle Bill used to have a cottage on the Sandusky River. It was just a short drive. To get to it, we had to turn off the main highway and travel almost a half mile on a gravel road. The posted speed limit was 5 MPH, and Dad never went faster than that. Because we always wanted to get to the cottage, it seemed excruciatingly slow. One day, Jeff said, "Why are you going so slow? We could *run* faster than this!"

Dad responded, "Do you think so? Well, go ahead. I'll keep it at the speed limit."

We couldn't believe it. He *never* let us do things like that. Run along the road? Really? Even though there was literally no traffic, it didn't seem like something he'd do. And no way would Mom go along with it. Yet, she did!

He stopped the car and let us out. Now, although 5 MPH seems slow when you're driving, it's pretty fast to run for a half mile, especially for little kids like us. But we were convinced we could do it.

Mom, Dad, Pat, and Cathy led in the car, and Jeff and I ran behind. Dad must've started out pretty slow, because we had no trouble keeping up. But then we started to fall back, just a little. Then a little more. But we kept it up. Yes, we were getting tired. Really tired. But we persisted. Still, we were falling back. Finally, the car was way ahead, and we realized we couldn't do it. Darn! We were sure we could outrun the car.

But it wasn't to be. And that was the end of it. Or so I thought.

As time went on, I completely forgot about it. Till one night. I'll have to explain.

Our house had no central heat. Instead, we had a couple floor furnaces, which were exactly what they sound like: furnaces in the floor covered by a grate. No ductwork, no fans, no blowers. Just these two furnaces that gave off a lot of heat. Although they heated the house, it wasn't exactly an even heat. But it was plenty warm near the furnaces. We used to stand on them all the time. Mom used to yell at us, "Don't stand on the furnace!" I guess she figured once we moved off, we'd be cold. (She was right.)

Upstairs? *No* heat upstairs. Well, almost none. In the living room ceiling were two openings between the downstairs ceiling and the bedroom floors upstairs. They were covered with grates we called "registers," about one foot square. As you can imagine, this didn't really let much heat up, so it was always cold up there. Our room wasn't too bad because it was directly above the furnace. But Pat's and Cathy's room was freezing. All winter long.

There was a side benefit to the registers. When we were supposed to be in bed, we could crawl on the floor to the register and look down to see what the adults were up to. Normally we couldn't see much, but we could *hear* things all the time. Mom and Dad kinda forgot about them, and they would talk like normal adults do. They didn't realize their kids might be listening.

No, I never heard any deep, dark secrets. But one night I heard Dad talk about the day Jeff and I tried to keep up with the car on the way to the cottage. He was laughing and laughing. Unknown to Jeff and I, Dad had *not* kept the car at the speed limit. He'd started slowly, then gradually sped up. Just enough at first to lead us along. But then he went faster and faster till we just couldn't do it anymore. And he thought it was the funniest thing!

I suppose I could have been mad. But somehow, it really wasn't a big deal. Did Dad lie to us? Well, kinda sorta. But the kind of lie we tell people when we play jokes. So no real big deal. And actually, it made me feel better. Because I had been *sure* I could keep up with the car. Looking back on it, maybe I'd been right all along.

If Dad hadn't cheated!

Kenny's Market

While it's probably misleading, we tend to remember the good things from "back in the old days" more than the bad. We definitely make the good things seem even better than they were. Were "the good old days" really better? That's for each of us to decide.

However, there is no doubt, at least to me, that some things from "the good old days" really were better. Corner grocery stores are one of those things.

I'm not talking about Dollar General, which seems to be everywhere today. And I'm not talking corporate stores. I'm talking real neighborhood grocery stores, run by just a few people. People who were your neighbors, who lived close by, who knew you, and whose sole income was from that store.

We had a number of those in my childhood. The closest one was Kenny's Market. It was just around the corner on Fifth Street, about a five-minute walk from our house. It was a tiny thing. Two very small aisles, plus a candy counter and a meat counter. Besides being the owner, Kenny was, apparently, a butcher as well. Or at least close enough to one that he could sell cuts of meat out of a butcher display case.

Mom didn't buy our weekly groceries there. I don't really think anyone did. That wasn't what it was for. But almost everyone in the neighborhood went there when they needed "just a few things." What's amazing about those times is that a store like that was enough to supply an honest living to Kenny. Plus, he had one or two employees. In today's economy, that would never work, but in my childhood things were different. People could make a living running a store like that, which is why they were common.

I didn't normally go to Kenny's for myself. But often Mom would send one of us kids to Kenny's to get something she needed. Maybe a can of beans, or a bag of sugar, or a loaf of bread. Things like that.

We'd go there and pick up those items. But of course, Mom didn't give us cash, and credit cards weren't common back then. When we bought something, Kenny would write it down on a pad of paper. In other words, we charged it. Each month, he'd have a bill for Mom, and she'd go in and pay it.

It was quite often I'd go there to buy something for Mom. If I had enough money of my own, I'd buy a candy bar or something for myself. But I didn't do that much.

In today's world, the idea of sending a six-year-old kid two or three blocks away, all by himself, to a store, without any money, to pick up a few things, is unheard of. For about a zillion reasons. But in the early 60s, this was common. We didn't think anything of it.

Of course, Kenny's isn't there anymore. The building still is. But now it's someone's residence. I've often wondered what it looks like inside. I can still picture the layout of that store. It really is hard to imagine it as a home. But it is.

One time, after Mom had been to Kenny's, she said she'd talked to him, and he said all us kids were really good kids. He said that unlike some kids, we didn't buy candy or things for ourselves and charge it. We only got what we were supposed to get. Mom was very pleased, of course. She loved it when someone praised her kids.

When she came home and told us what he'd said, the whole "We're really good kids" thing passed me by. All I could think was, *You mean I could have charged candy and pop and things like that? Really?* You see, it wasn't really that I was a good kid. It was more that, apparently, I wasn't very smart. Because I never even thought about charging candy. All that time I could have been charging things like that, and I *never even thought about it!* Apparently, I did *not* have a criminal mind.

Looking back, I don't know if I would've done that even if I had thought about it. While Kenny didn't give Mom an itemized bill, I'm sure she'd have figured it out eventually. Mom always seemed able to figure out things like that.

Still, that was the first time in my life I realized I didn't think like a criminal. All in all, I guess that's a good thing.

My Paper Route, Part 1

When we used to play outside in the summer, sometime in the afternoon, we'd hear Davey's mom yell for him, about the same time Gordy's mom yelled for him. That meant it was time for their paper routes.

I always thought it would be really cool to have a paper route. Maybe because I could make my own money. But more likely, it was just because the older kids delivered papers. And little kids always want to be "older."

When I was in third grade or so, I got my paper route. Actually, I got Davey's paper route. Or half of it anyway. He outgrew it, so he gave it to Jeff and me to split up. We each had about thirty customers.

I remember the first day I got my route. I took my delivery bag to school and hung it up with my coat. I told the teacher, "I'll be bringing that to school from now on, because I have a paper route." I tried to say it real nonchalant and cool. But I'm pretty sure Miss Battiste could see that I was pretty proud. Because *I had a job*! I was working! I was making money! Just like an adult. Honestly, I felt pretty cool.

Well, having a job sounded like a whole lot more fun than it actually was. It wasn't too bad during the school year, because we'd go right from school to the paper office, pick up our papers, deliver them, and be done. (At least that's how it was supposed to go.) But during the summer, we'd be out playing when Mom would call us for our paper routes. I hated that. I wanted to keep playing. But the papers had to be delivered, so I'd go. Even if I didn't want to.

We had to ride our bikes to the Daily News office on Fifth Street. The newspaper was housed in a relatively small building that held all the offices, writers, ad reps, and others. Attached was the garage. *That's* where the paperboys went to get their papers. That's where the printing press was; that's where the paper was made. The wall had clothespins that held our route numbers, any notices they needed to give us, and the bills that showed how much we owed for the papers that week.

To be honest, the newspaper office was pretty cool because of the garage with that printing press. The thing was magical. Huge rolls of paper were fed through the machine, and it seemed like it went so fast. The paper got unrolled, ran through a pretty complicated path, stretched a zillion different ways, and got printed on, then folded and stacked. And this wasn't a printer; it was a press. It was *loud.* And it had real metal type. At least that's how I remember it.

One time when I was in the office waiting for my papers, the boss lady was talking to me about "type." Now, maybe I'm remembering it wrong, but I swear to God the whole paper was printed with little bits of metal type, each letter having its own little piece of metal. These were arranged, by hand, by some guys whose job it was to do that—which means they put the whole paper together while reading backward. Because of course you had to set the type backward so when it printed it came out right. The boss was telling me how some of the guys there could read backward just as well as reading forward.

Honestly, I can't believe I'm remembering it right. Seems an odd way to print a paper. Yet, that's what's in my head.

I don't think I was a particularly good paperboy. In fact, I'm sure I wasn't. Oh, I delivered the papers, but not always in a timely manner. For instance, some kids about my age would play football in their yard. Now, how was I supposed to just ride on by? That was impossible for me. So, right in the middle of my route, I'd stop for an hour or so.

Also, the gas station gave me trouble. There wasn't anything wrong with it. But I used to stop in there, sit around, waste time, and talk to the guys working there. (You'd have thought I'd grow up to be a car guy, but that never happened.)

My route included a laundromat as well. There's nothing exciting about a laundromat, except that in the winter when I was freezing, it was warm. *And* it had a hot chocolate machine. I could go into the laundromat to warm up, put a dime in the machine, and get a cup of hot chocolate. I'd milk that time for quite a while. I didn't really want to go back out into the cold.

The fastest way to deliver the papers was to roll them up with a rubber band, then throw them on porches. I had back baskets on my bike, so when I did this, I could get the route done really quick. But that meant I had to take all…that…time…rolling the papers. I mean, how long could it have taken to roll thirty papers? Somehow it took me forever. Sometimes

MY PAPER ROUTE, PART I

I just folded them. But they tended to fly apart when I threw them, so I didn't do that often.

I also was a little...scatterbrained. Sometimes I'd get home with a couple extra papers. Which meant I'd forgotten someone. Usually they'd call, and I'd have to ride back to give them the paper. Or sometimes I'd miss the porch. If it was in the bushes, I'd go pick it up. But there were times I threw it on the roof! I just kinda rode away, hoping they wouldn't care. There really wasn't much I could do. I don't really think they wanted me to climb up on their roof!

As I said, if I forgot a customer, sometimes they'd call. At the time I couldn't figure it out. I mean, so you miss the newspaper once in a while? But now, as an adult, I understand how messing with a routine isn't always ideal. If they counted on reading the paper after dinner and it wasn't there, I can, looking back at least, understand why they'd call.

Actually, though, calling wasn't too bad. It was much worse when they called the newspaper office. I hated that. Because every day when we walked into the garage to get our papers, we'd check the wall with the clothespins. I had number 27. And I hated it when I walked in and saw a pink slip hanging there. That meant there was a complaint. Ugh. I have to admit, I don't ever remember getting into trouble because of a complaint, but I still didn't like it.

It really is a shame that paperboys and papergirls don't exist much today. Of course, almost nobody gets a real paper anymore. But even twenty years ago, when we *did* still read papers, there were almost no kids delivering them. Sometimes we had a papergirl, but even then her mom drove her for her route, pretty much every day. Mostly, it was adults delivering from their car, and we paid them online or by mail. We didn't ever get to know that person.

While being a paperboy wasn't always fun and games, I think it helped me understand responsibility and work. Also, it allowed me to interact with adults as a kinda-sorta equal, rather than just a kid. And yes, I made a little money.

All these were good lessons. At least I think they were.

My Paper Route, Part 2

We delivered the paper Monday through Friday. On Saturday, we'd collect. Which meant I had to knock on every single door and ask for the fifty cents it cost for the week. No paying online or sending a check for us. The way we did it was so old school. The newspaper owners understood that eight-year-old kids were not the best at writing receipts. Instead, we had a card for each customer on a metal ring, with the dates for all the Saturdays of the year for each customer. Each customer had an identical card. We also had a paper punch. Instead of a normal round punch, ours made diamonds, or hearts, or some other random shape. When customers paid, we punched their card and ours. So that was a kind of receipt, I guess.

That took forever, it seemed, and when I was done, I had to pay my bill. I'd ride my bike to the National Bank and go to the window designated as the "paper boys pay here" window. I'd pay what I owed for the papers, and the rest was profit.

Unfortunately, I wasn't really great at business. I was supposed to make two cents for each paper. So thirty papers for five days is 150 papers, or three dollars per week. That doesn't sound like much today, but I was used to getting a dime each week for my allowance, so this was huge. But somehow it never seemed to work out that way. And I never really did figure out why.

Part of the problem, I think, was that I wasn't a good bookkeeper. (To be fair, I was only eight years old!) Actually, we didn't keep books at all. As I said, we just punched the customer's card. If we didn't punch it, it meant they hadn't paid.

But somehow it never worked out. My friend Andy was way more organized. When someone paid ahead, he'd put that "extra" money in a jar till the next week. Me? I have no idea what I did with it. All I know is that I never seemed to make the profit I was supposed to. Alas.

Sure, I'd spend some of it. For instance, every Saturday after I had paid my bill at the National Bank, I went down the street to Timblin's drug store. It had a soda fountain. And it was pretty cool. I always got the same thing: a Green River and a packet of Lance cheese and peanut butter crackers. It cost me twenty-five cents. Yes, that was some of my profit, but a small amount. And no, I'm not exactly sure what a Green River was, except it was a sweet green fizzy drink that came in a Coke glass. I loved Green Rivers. I haven't had one in years. But the Lance crackers? I still eat them.

After Timblin's, I'd ride my bike to the Western Auto store, which had a huge display case of Matchbox cars. Each week I'd treat myself to one. They cost forty-nine cents at first, but went up to fifty-five cents after a year or so.

Yes, those all cost money, but they were one of the highlights of my week. I bought them with my own money. I honestly felt so adult!

I eventually had quite a collection of those Matchbox cars. They're gone now, sadly. They should have aged well, but Mom always got them out when someone with kids came to visit. Eventually, they were all lost or broken. Sad, but completely understandable.

Looking back on it, I wonder what my customers thought of me. I wasn't always prompt, but for the most part, they got their papers. Eventually. Also I was pretty friendly, and I always talked to the customers when I saw them. I knew them all. Mr. Wilson used to give me a ten-cent tip. He'd tell me, "Go buy a beer. A root beer, that is." And Mr. Ward used to wash his car all the time. I remember Mrs. Taylor used to sing a lot. In other words, we knew each other.

But I'm sure sometimes they heard me singing, or talking to myself while playing some imaginary scenario in my head.

I'm guessing they mostly just laughed. At least that's what I hope.

My Paper Route, Part 3

I don't know if it was to teach us something or because of a lack of time, but neither of my parents ever drove me on my route—with one notable exception. It was pouring rain, and I was walking instead of riding my bike for some reason. There was lightning all around me. (Yes, really!) A smart kid would've waited it out on someone's porch, I suppose. But I kept delivering. Well, I was completely soaked (and I'm guessing the papers were as well), but as I was walking away from a house on Laurel Avenue, lightning struck pretty much right next to me.

I immediately wet my pants. Which is *very* embarrassing for a third grader. Luckily, Laurel Avenue was the closest part of my route to my house, so I walked home. (Crying, I'm sure.) And after I changed into clean, dry clothes, Mom drove me to deliver the rest of my papers. Pretty sure that was the only time I got a ride.

Also, delivering papers was a solitary activity. I could never talk any of my friends into coming with me. The one who came with me a lot was our dog, Rusty. Rusty would tag along on my route. She learned it pretty well after a while. She never got lost, she never ran in front of a car, and she never bit or barked at anyone.

But there was one day. A very bad day. I don't know what prompted it, but one of the guys on my route went after Rusty with a metal garden rake. I still remember it. I don't think he was one of my customers. He wore one of those work shirts with his name on an oval patch above the left pocket. And he hit Rusty with the rake, and really hurt her.

Of course, I cried, then picked Rusty up and somehow got her home on my bike. We took her to the vet, and it turned out she had a broken leg. They patched her up pretty well, and she eventually recovered completely. But for the rest of her life, whenever she saw a man wearing work clothes with a name patch, she went crazy. Other people she'd leave alone. But for anyone dressed like her attacker, she went nuts.

For what it's worth, when that man hit Rusty, I was really upset. I kept crying and crying. Mom said to me, "Remember when I broke my leg a few years ago? You didn't cry when it happened to me, but you're crying for Rusty."

It was true. I think the difference was that I watched it happen to Rusty, but with Mom I came upon the scene after the fact. I'm sure Mom understood that. I think her point was to get me to realize that she was okay, and Rusty would be as well.

Rusty was fine after that. Once she recovered, she continued to help me with my paper route. She didn't actually deliver any papers of course, but she kept me company. She did that as long as I had the route.

Eventually, when I got to junior high and I had sports after school, I quit the route. Three years or so was all it was, but it was an essential part of my childhood.

I wish kids had that opportunity today.

Grandpa Jack and Grandma Dutch

My dad was born in 1927. Shortly after his birth, his mother died of appendicitis. His dad, Grandpa Whitey, was a nineteen-year old kid left with an infant. Today there might be lots of choices for him. In 1927, not so much.

His mother's family took Dad, but when Dad's other grandma and grandpa went to visit once, Grandma Dutch (real name Ruby) reportedly said, "He's too skinny. We have to fatten him up," and took him home with her. (Remember, this was 1927. No courts or lawyers; she just took him.) Consequently, Dad was raised by his paternal grandpa and grandma—Grandpa Jack and Grandma Dutch.

We always loved going to visit Grandpa Jack and Grandma Dutch. Grandpa was a commercial fisherman, and going to their house was pretty cool, especially as they got older. When they were aging, instead of a house on the highway, they moved into a small mobile home on Aunt Mabel's property. The reason it was fun was because it was right where their fishing business was located. They had a bunch of ugly gray fishing boats docked on Beef Creek (pronounced "crick"). And there was a "carp pond" where Grandpa threw all the fish he didn't want. Not all fish could be sold, and carp were one of them.

Jeff and I used to go fishing in the creek and the carp pond. (I don't remember catching much though.) We never swam in the pond that I remember, but we went ice skating a lot in the winter. Sometimes the ice would make cracking noises, and we'd get real scared, but Dad assured us it was just the ice expanding, and we'd be safe. Which we were.

Eventually, Grandma Dutch suffered badly from dementia and passed away. Grandpa Jack, however, lived quite a bit longer. I remember going to visit him. He had a tiny twelve-inch black-and-white TV that got three channels. He sat in his recliner and watched it all day, from what I could tell. Somehow, it always seemed he watched a lot of *Divorce Court*, or at least that's how I remember. He also smoked Camels, no filters, pretty much nonstop. His fingers took on a permanent brownish-yellow tint from them.

One time, he became ill, so Mom brought him to our house to stay for a few weeks till he recovered. I have no idea where he slept, because our house was very tiny. I mostly remember I had to learn to tie certain knots for Cub Scouts. I just couldn't get them—until Grandpa Jack showed me. As a fisherman, I think he knew just about every knot ever tied! And he was actually a great teacher. I learned those knots in no time.

Eventually, of course, he passed away. Periodically I drive out to where that trailer was situated and try to imagine how it was when I was young. Somehow, I just can't. Mabel's house is still there, but the mobile home is gone. It's a marina now, so the carp pond is connected to the creek and filled with docks for boats. I think they've filled in some areas and dredged others, because it's so different. Still, if I try, I can stand there and imagine fishing in the creek, or skating on the pond, or talking to Grandpa while he was smoking Camels and watching TV.

Somehow, those memories still take me back.

Herman

Snowball the rabbit with Herman, the duck

Us boys used to roam all over the neighborhood. One boy, Bob, lived a few streets over. Because he was a little farther away, he wasn't in our regular group of friends. But once in a while we'd get together. And Bob always liked to go to the railroad tracks.

A set of railroad tracks goes right through our town. They're raised so traffic can go underneath them. They're probably about twenty-five feet high, but they're built on a bunch of dirt piled up, rather than concrete. Which means they're easy to climb. We didn't go there much, because they were a few blocks away. But Bob, living closer, went there all the time. He liked to catch snakes there.

One day, we all decided to go to the railroad tracks to catch snakes. We even took one of Mom's canning jars with us, which was unusual. Normally we just caught them and put them in our pockets. But this time we were going to save them I guess.

Davey, Gordy, Johnny, Bob, Jeff, and I all climbed the railroad tracks in search of garter snakes. Garter snakes aren't very big, and are completely harmless. Sometimes they were out in the open; sometimes they'd hide under rocks. They weren't hard to find. Within a short time, we had three or four snakes in the jar. Time to head home.

This must have happened shortly after Easter, because on the way home, we came across two little kids playing with a tiny duckling. In the 60s, some stores sold little chicks and ducklings, sometimes dyed bright colors. People would buy them and take them home, what, as pets? That never made any real sense to me, but that's what happened. These two kids had one of those ducklings. He was tiny, just a few inches long. They asked what was in the jar, so we showed them. Well, apparently, they thought snakes were pretty cool, because they asked us to trade the snakes for the duck.

Heck, we could catch more snakes any time we wanted, so we made the deal. Now, we all owned a duck.

We had no idea how this was going to work, but we decided we would share the duck, with each kid having him for a week. Since there were two Morgans, Jeff and I, we got him first. I'm sure Mom was very pleased. Okay, maybe not.

First, we had to give him a name. Somehow, we chose "Herman."

When we got home, we took Herman all over the neighborhood, showing him off and putting him in all the little neighborhood backyard kiddie pools. To this day, I don't understand why, but Herman started shivering. Bad. Who knew ducks could shiver? But he did. We were really worried. We didn't want Herman to die.

Mom tried to help. First she turned the oven on low and set Herman in front of it. But that didn't seem to work, so she got her hair dryer out. Blow dryers weren't a thing yet, but she had one of those with a plastic bonnet you set over your hair. We put Herman in the bonnet and turned it on low. That did the trick. Very shortly, Herman was doing just fine.

I don't remember what we fed him, but I know he was not a "house duck." And I know we never gave him up to the other kids. They never asked, either. So he was our duck.

And Herman thrived. He grew and grew. Grandpa Clarence built a pen for Herman, and sometimes he'd stay in it. At that time I also had a pet rabbit, Snowball. We put Snowball and Herman in that pen once, but Herman kept biting Snowball's ears, so that only happened once. Even though there was a pen, mostly we just let Herman roam free. And he did. All over the yard. His favorite place to sit when it was hot was under Mom's car, because it was shaded. Poor Snowball, however, was stuck back in his cage. Honestly, looking back, I feel bad for Snowball. We never let him out to run, and I almost never picked him up or petted him. It had to be a very lonely life for Snowball. I really should have paid more attention to him!

That year, we went on a vacation to the Smoky Mountains, and we were gone for two weeks. We left Herman in the care of a neighbor boy (*not* one of the ones was with us when we got Herman.) Toward the end of the vacation, Dad said, "We're done in the Smokies and are heading home. We can go right home, or we can stop at Mammoth Cave. You guys decide." I voted to go home, because I really, really missed Herman. I'm not sure why the others voted as they did, but we came right home.

I couldn't wait to go get Herman. But when I did, I hardly recognized him. He had grown quite a bit, and all his yellow pinfeathers were gone. Herman was no longer a duckling. He was a big, white, duck!

The summer progressed, and we had to face that come winter, we couldn't keep a duck. We were afraid he'd freeze, or something. We had no idea how this was going to end.

One day, one very bad day, that decision was made for us. Mom came out in the backyard and told us she was running some errands. My sisters were to look after us little kids. Besides the four of us, some other child was also with us. I can't remember who he was, but he was younger than me. Shortly after Mom left, he came to me and said, "Herman's dead."

Well, Herman slept a lot, so I figured he was sleeping. And I said so.

But the kid said, "No, he's really dead. I'll show you." He took me to the alley next to our house and showed me.

There, in a mess of blood, guts, and feathers, was Herman. Or what was left of him.

Honestly, it was horrible. I cried. I screamed. I went a little crazy probably. I *loved* Herman, and he wasn't just dead; he was smashed. Completely. We couldn't even recognize him. I couldn't stop crying. Neither could Jeff. We were distraught. Pat and Cathy did what they could, but we just kept crying.

Finally Mom came home, and Pat told her what had happened. She told Mom, "Jeff and Dick won't stop crying. I keep slapping them, but it doesn't help." Apparently, she'd seen that on TV somewhere. But no, it didn't work.

Eventually, of course, we got control of ourselves. I have no recollection of who cleaned Herman up or what they did with him. But Mom knew she had most likely run Herman over. By where we found him, it was clear Herman had been sleeping under Mom's car like he always did, and tried to run to escape when she drove away. Unfortunately, he didn't make it.

Mom knew what she had done. And felt horrible. But even in our grief, we knew it wasn't really her fault.

As sad as that was, it kept us from deciding what we were going to do with him come winter. We had all kinds of ideas, but of course they all involved letting Herman go somewhere—somewhere that wasn't our home. It would have been hard to give him up. As traumatic as this experience was, it at least made that decision for us.

And you know, he was only a duck. Not a dog or cat. But I still kinda miss Herman. He was a good duck.

Carp Hunting

Port Clinton was a great town to be a kid. It was big enough that there was always some new place to explore. But it was small enough that we could ride our bikes wherever we wanted. And it's right on the Lake Erie shore, where the Portage River empties into the lake.

We could go down to the water's edge whenever we wanted. Sometimes we went to the beach, but more commonly we went to the pier. The pier was a pile of rocks built into a kind of wall that formed a channel for the Portage River as it emptied into Lake Erie.

Right beside that pier, at the lake's shore, was the marsh, a swampy area with lots of water plants. For some reason, carp thrived there.

If you don't know anything about carp, they're big, slow, fish. They can be ten inches long, or they can be almost three feet long. Bottom feeders, I'm pretty sure. Most carp are gray, but sometimes they're orange. Basically, they're huge goldfish. In the murky water, the gray ones were hard to spot. But the orange ones stood out.

So we used to go carp hunting. I have no idea what we did with the carp when we caught them. They're not considered good eating, although Grandpa Clarence used to smoke them sometimes in his smoker. But that's not why we caught them. We did it because it was fun.

I remember one time vividly. We were home from school on spring break. Lake Erie, in those days, was covered with ice all winter long. During spring break, the water was way too cold for swimming. But kids are tough about those things. We went in.

Now, how do you catch carp? Of course you can use a fishing pole, but we were "hunting," not "fishing." So we had a variety of methods.

Davey had a frog spear. It looked like a little pitchfork, with five very sharp tines about six inches long. The plan was to throw it at the carp, hoping to skewer it. But most of us didn't have spears. The rest of us used baseball bats, shovels, or anything we could use as a club. We used these to try to bash the carp. And Jeff could catch them with his hands. Really. He was the only one who could do it.

This time, about five of us went down to the pier and climbed into the water. It had to be freezing, but we went in anyway. We wandered around till someone flushed out a carp and yelled, "*Carp!*"

We all ran after the carp. Most of us were swinging our makeshift clubs. Davey threw his spear. Jeff caught them with his hands.

I'm trying to picture that. It's probably a good thing Mom didn't really know what we were doing. Imagine seeing a bunch of elementary-aged kids, running all over in the freezing water. With some of them swinging baseball bats, and one throwing a spear, it really is a wonder nobody ever got hurt. But I can guarantee if any of our moms had seen it, we'd have been done.

Yeah, looking back on it, it was pretty dangerous. But we survived it. Which is more than I can say for the carp.

My Piano Teacher's Cat

As I've said, I took piano lessons. But I haven't talked about the teacher's cat.

She had this cat named Petey. I don't remember much about him; I think he was black, with short hair. Like all cats, he climbed on things: the couch, the piano, the windowsill, etc.

One day, when I sat down at her piano for my lesson, I happened to glance out the window, and on the windowsill was a pile of cat poop. Honest. Well, at least I thought it was cat poop. But Mrs. Andrews didn't seem to notice it. So I didn't say a thing. I mean, what if it was some weird decoration, and I told her it was cat poop? Yes, I know most decorations don't look like cat poop. But I was only seven or eight then, and I really wasn't sure. So I figured it was best to not say anything. I figured she'd see it pretty soon and clean it up. It was only about two feet from where she sat.

Trying not to think about the poop, I finished the lesson and rode my bike home. When I went back a week later for my next lesson, I was pretty sure the poop would be gone. But it wasn't! Really! There it was, still sitting in the same place on the windowsill. Really? Maybe it *was* a decoration after all. But I really couldn't figure out why anyone would have a decoration that looked like cat poop. Then again, I was a kid. And adults normally confused me anyway.

That went on for a number of weeks. I told myself it really was a decoration. An ugly decoration, but it *had* to be. As I remember it, her house was pretty clean. So of course, she couldn't have just missed it.

Then one day, when I went to my lesson, it was *gone*. The poop was gone. So I guess it really was poop. Of course I never asked her about it. But I've always wondered what went through her head when she saw it. I'd have been so embarrassed, knowing all my piano students had come into my house, and probably saw that pile. On the other hand, maybe when she saw it, she thought it was new.

I didn't know, and I didn't ask.

Luckily, it never happened again. Either Petey learned his lesson, or Mrs. Andrews was more diligent. Either way, I was glad the poop was gone.

Cocoa

Most of the family enjoying Grandpa Clarence's hot cocoa: Grandpa Clarence, Grandma Marvel, Uncle Bill, Pat, Jeff, Cathy, Dick, and Dad

Every family has traditions, and ours was no exception. In fact, we had a lot of them. Some were new traditions that started in our lifetimes, so we knew how they'd come about. But some were just...the way it had always been. We had no idea how those got started.

One of the traditions I loved had to do with Grandpa Clarence. And no, I have no idea where this tradition came from.

Back then, every church had a huge Sunday school. Each year, the Sunday school kids put on a Christmas program. I'm sure you've seen things like this. Each kid dressed up, maybe as shepherds or wise men or angels. Or maybe even donkeys or sheep. Then each kid learned a part, maybe a line or two, and recited it at the program. Almost always, they reenacted the nativity. They were always very predictable, but also very cute.

These were big deals for us kids. Of course Mom and Dad came, but so did Grandma and Grandpa. We were always nervous for these programs, but usually we got through them okay. Whether we did or didn't, our grandparents always said we were wonderful. And we always believed them.

Okay, that's not tradition. That's just what every elementary-aged kid went through in the 60s. The tradition came afterward. Once the program was all over and we had greeted all our "fans" and could finally relax, we went back home.

That's where Grandpa made his famous hot cocoa. Now let's be honest here. This was the 60s. Most men in the 60s didn't cook. At all. I know Grandpa Clarence didn't cook. Yet each Christmas Eve, he made his famous hot cocoa. We all looked forward to it.

Why? Was it better than, say, Nestle's Quik? (Although it's now called "Nesquik," in my head, it was and always will be "Nestle's Quik.") Probably not. But it was *Grandpa's*! So we really anticipated it, and loved it.

As you can imagine, Mom probably did most of the work. I'm sure she bought all the ingredients, got out all the necessary pots and pans, and arranged the mugs on the counter. But Grandpa was the one who mixed it all together, so he was the one who got the credit.

I don't remember every year, but I do have memories of at least a few years of this. I even remember which pot he used. It made an impression on me. After being so nervous for so long for the Christmas program, us kids could come home, sit down, and drink Grandpa's cocoa.

I don't have his recipe anymore. Maybe he just used the one on the Hershey's Cocoa container. I have no idea. But it was good enough. It was a tradition we loved. Partly because of the cocoa.

But probably also because we loved Grandpa. And he loved doing it.

Pears... and More

Grandpa Clarence was a common laborer. No college degree, and maybe even not a high school diploma. I really have no idea. He always had a job, sometimes very well paying, in some factory or other.

But his first love was farming. If he'd had his way, he'd have been a farmer his whole life. But, at least from the stories told to me, Grandma Marvel was in no way, shape, or form going to be a "farm wife." The story was that she told him something to the effect of, "You can marry me, or you can be a farmer, but you can't do both."

I hope Grandma didn't do that. While I understand her thoughts I guess, it just seems really not nice of her to deny Grandpa what he wanted to do. But for whatever reason, Grandpa was not a farmer.

That didn't mean he couldn't have a garden. He definitely had a garden. Two, actually: a small one in his backyard, and a much bigger one somewhere else, on a friend's farm I think. And he planted a lot.

Besides the garden, he had a number of fruit trees. I don't think he had apples, but I know he had peaches and pears.

Grandpa loved growing all this stuff. And harvesting it. But really, what was he going to do with it? It was just him,

PEARS... AND MORE

Grandma, and my Uncle Bill in that house. They could only eat so much. Instead of letting it go to waste, he put it in his truck and took it to his two daughters, Mom and her sister, Aunt Annie.

One afternoon, Grandpa drove up, pulled down the tailgate, and removed a number of bushel baskets of pears. This wasn't unusual. Quite often he'd come by with bushel baskets of peas, beans, corn, cucumbers, peaches, and more. He was so happy to give it all to Mom and Aunt Annie.

Well, that sounds good, but really, what does a mother of four do with bushels of produce? (If you don't know how big a bushel is, well, it's a lot of pears!) Maybe today we'd freeze it all. But we didn't have a freezer, at least not when I was real young. Besides, freezing pears doesn't really work well.

Instead, Mom canned them.

As you may know, "canning" is a misnomer. You don't use cans; you use jars. Since Mom had four kids, she didn't use pints or half-pints. No, Mom was strictly a quart jar kind of canner. In fact, she canned so much that Dad had one of his friends build a whole wall of cabinets in the laundry room. They were about five feet tall, three feet deep, and probably 12 feet wide. Mom filled a good part of that with canned goods. While she canned a lot of things, the ones I remember most are pickles, peaches, and pears.

It wasn't till I was much older that Mom confessed that, while she loved her father and was very grateful for his produce gifts, she sometimes wished he didn't bring them. Canning that much is a *lot* of work. With four kids, and working quite a bit at the hospital, she only had so much time.

The produce she dreaded the most was pears. Apparently, there is no easy way to peel pears. Peaches are kinda like tomatoes; if you heat them for a very short time in boiling water, the peels slip off. (If you want to sound like you know what you're talking about, the term for this process is "blanching.") But blanching wasn't a thing for pears, at least according to Mom. Instead, she had to peel them with a peeler or knife. If Grandpa brought her two bushels of them, think about how long that had to take her.

But she didn't let them rot. No, she was a good daughter and a good mom, and canned them all. I really loved her canned pears. Sometimes I sat down and ate pear after pear after pear. I liked the peaches too, but the pears really were my favorite.

Except maybe for pickles. Mom had a sweet pickle recipe she got from JoJo, the very nice, very helpful neighbor. I still have her recipe, and while I don't need to go into all the details, the first step was to soak cucumbers in salt water for more than two weeks. It was common in late summer to have a huge crock filled with cucumbers soaking for weeks. (And yes, in case you don't know, pickles are just small cucumbers that have been "pickled.") These cucumbers, while soaking, got a thick layer of mold all over the surface of the salt water. It looked gross and deadly, but it was part of the process.

All of this canning was an incredible amount of work, which is one reason so few do it anymore. But Mom did. Because Grandpa brought her the stuff. And because it saved a whole lot of money. And because her kids liked the stuff she canned. And also, probably, because it was expected.

I have recently started canning as well. I can tomatoes and tomato sauce, but I'm most proud of the pickles. Yes, I still use JoJo's recipe. And yes, it's a whole lot of work. And yes, I still love them. Apparently, it's an acquired taste, because most people aren't quite as crazy about them as I am. Except for my Grandson Zane, who loves them. In fact, that's what I give him for his birthday. And he's always thrilled.

Gotta admit though, while I love the pickles, I do it mostly because Mom did. Somehow it feels like I'm honoring her whenever I can anything. I no longer work full time, but instead have a number of part-time jobs. I don't have any kids at home. Still, when I can them, I'm amazed at how much time it takes.

But Mom did probably twenty times the amount of canning I do, and she had a part-time job and four kids at home. And she somehow found the time.

Even for the pears.

Age 9 and 10

Mom's Wisdom, Part 2

I'm not exactly sure how old I was, but I know I wasn't ten yet. For my birthday coming up at the end of September, I asked for a bow and arrow. (Okay, maybe a couple of arrows!) Davey from across the street had a bow. He showed me how to hold it, string it, and shoot it. He gave me all the safety warnings, and I felt ready. So I asked Mom and Dad for a bow and arrow.

For the time being, let's forget that in today's world, not too many parents would buy a nine-year-old who lived in town a bow and arrows. It seems kind of irresponsible actually. But the world was different in 1965, and honestly, I don't think safety was even a consideration.

Anyway, I asked, I begged, I pleaded. And weeks before my birthday, a long thin package showed up in the kitchen. It was all wrapped up with a bow, leaning in the corner by the steps, and it obviously was the bow and arrows. Jeff said that the present was from him, and it wasn't a bow. Yeah right! I knew he was covering, trying to keep it a surprise.

Of course, I was really impatient. And excited. I couldn't wait, just couldn't wait. It took *forever*, but finally, my birthday came, and I politely opened the other packages first. I saved the best for last. When it was time, I opened the long thin package.

I couldn't wait to open my bow. As I tore into it, I saw that it was—a fishing pole.

I had been sure it was a bow, yet there was a fishing pole where the bow and arrows should have been. I was decimated, to say the least. I'd been sure I was getting a bow. In my nine-year-old brain, I deserved the bow.

What happened next, I remember vividly. I looked at my brother and said, "Thanks, Jeff; I can really use a new fishing pole." And truthfully, I *did* need a new pole. My old one was definitely for little kids. This fishing pole was way better. Yes, I was disappointed, but for some reason, I kept it together, and didn't complain at all.

Then, and only then, Mom said, "Oh, I just remembered, there's one more present out in the trunk of the car. Here's my keys."

I took her keys, ran out to the driveway, opened the trunk, and there, not even wrapped, were the bow and arrows I had wanted all along. Woo Hoo!

To this day, I don't know how or why I held it together, why I didn't whine and complain. After all, I was a kid, and like all kids, I did my share of that. I'm not sure. Maybe it was because I really did need a fishing pole. Or maybe it was because Jeff was obviously proud that he had bought his little brother such a good present. Or maybe it was because Mom and Dad had taught me that lesson before. I don't know.

But here's the thing. I never asked her, but I'm sure Mom kept that present in her car for a reason. There's no way she "forgot." I'll never know for sure, but I'd bet anything that if I had whined, fussed, or complained about not getting the bow, that bow and arrows would have gone right back to the store. I will always believe she withheld it to test me, and to teach me. It was a lesson taught, and learned, that I didn't even know I was getting. It wasn't till years later that I realized the responsibility and sense of Mom's actions that day.

Just another example of Mom's wisdom.

Sohio

There used to be a gas station near our home. Actually, there were two gas stations. I've already written about Kelly's. But there was another one, called Clair Nau's, a little farther away. They sold penny candy. We didn't go there much, because Kelly's was closer. But we did go there once every couple of weeks.

Well, I don't know if we all went, but I remember Cathy and I going there. The gas station was a Sohio station. That brand doesn't exist anymore. It was part of Standard Oil (Standard Oil Ohio, or Sohio), but that doesn't really matter.

What does matter is that they used to have giveaways. Each week or so, they put a sheet of credit card numbers, or sometimes license numbers, in the window. If your number was shown, you won something. I have no idea what, because we never won.

Cathy and I walked down there quite often to check the numbers in the window. I suppose Mom could have written them down for us, but she didn't. We memorized them.

Now, I know what you're thinking: they posted *credit card* numbers? Yes, they did. Not exactly something we'd do today. But back then, identity theft wasn't a thing. They really did post those numbers. And Dad had a Sohio credit card. It had to be Dad, because in the early 1960s, women weren't allowed to have credit cards. (Which still amazes me!)

The odd thing is, I don't remember our license plate number, probably because each year we got a new one. I know it ended with a *P*, because almost all the Port Clinton plates ended with a *P*. But to this day, I still remember that credit card number. Cathy and I repeated it so much, apparently, that it's burned into our brains. Cathy passed away recently, sadly. But I remember talking to her about this a few years ago, and she remembered the number as well.

No, we never won. Although on a side note, for a while, Sohio sold china. Yes, china, Like plates and stuff. I remember Mom got her "good china" from Sohio.

Gas station china. Who would have guessed?

Even though we didn't win, I remember feeling important that I got to go check on it. I had my big sister with me, but still I felt cool that Mom trusted me with that job. So even though we didn't win, I didn't care. Because I felt like a "big kid."

And that was pretty cool.

Tent Sales

Tent Sale for Morgan's TV and Appliance

My dad had lots of jobs before I was born. He had a two-year engineering degree, paid for with the G.I. Bill after World War II. At first he worked at a local electronics factory, but he eventually started to repair televisions, radios, phonographs, and more on the side. He even installed forty to fifty-foot-tall antenna towers.

Sometime when I was a baby, he started a small business, a tiny store called Morgan's TV Sales and Service. He sold TVs, record players, records, and things like that. This was in the early 60s before color TV was a thing. I remember him telling me how difficult it was to keep records by The Beatles in stock—like impossible. Girls would come in looking for them, but they were always sold out. Still, he allowed them to listen to other records. (I don't think most record stores did that.) But mostly, they wanted The Beatles. Alas.

After a few years in this small store, he moved his store into a *much* larger building, added kitchen appliances to his stock, and renamed it Morgan's TV and Appliance. It was very successful. He had two big sales a year. The one I remember most was his summer "tent sale."

No, he didn't sell tents. He had a huge circus tent erected in the parking lot, moved a bunch of TVs and kitchen appliances out there, and for a week had a huge sale. He did it up completely. And advertised like crazy.

To me, the best part was he gave out free helium balloons, popcorn, and Coke. And he let *me* run that part of it. I was only about nine or ten at the time.

It was great. I spent the whole week there. I learned to tie balloons, and I learned the best way to loop the end so I could put the balloon around a kid's wrist and it wouldn't fly away. I got to make popcorn in one of those huge concession stand popcorn makers. And by far, the coolest part was that I got to drink all the Coke I wanted. Because it wasn't in bottles or cans. No, it was from a fountain Coke machine. Just pull the tap and the Coke poured out.

I know that doesn't seem like a big deal. I mean, any fast-food restaurant today has a serve-yourself soda machine. But back then, it was huge. In the 60s, most of us didn't drink

TENT SALES

much pop. Because honestly, it cost too much. Mom always made us Kool-Aid, but Coke or Pepsi was really a special treat. Even when we did get some, pop bottles back then were really, really small. Most varieties came in an eight-ounce bottle. 7UP was in a seven-ounce bottle. (Of course.) And those weirdly shaped Coke bottles were 6.5 ounces. Really. Now, most bottles are a minimum of about 16 ounces. Many are larger. And fast food sodas are sometimes twenty-four to forty ounces. *Not* 6.5.

So when I got to drink all the Coke I wanted, it was like heaven. The machine cooled the Coke, so we didn't have to bother with ice. My job was to dispense Coke into paper Coke cups, and serve them. *And* drink them myself. It was wonderful.

To this day, my favorite way to drink Coke is in a paper cup, with no ice. It reminds me of those tent sales.

This is an example of how we remember things from our childhoods being much bigger than they actually were. I remember that tent being *huge*, like you could put a circus in it. But that building and parking lot are still there, and the parking lot fits about six cars max. That's all. Yes, the tent could hold about twelve TVs and maybe twenty appliances when we crammed them all in there. It was *not* circus-size.

But it was to me. To me it was huge, and it was magical. Everything about those tent sales brings back good memories. Partly because I could drink all the Coke I wanted. But also because I was actually in charge of something. I felt very important. I was just a kid handing out free stuff. But to me, it was a responsibility. My dad actually thought I could handle it. And I did. It was nice to be given that responsibility. It was nice to be able to accomplish it. And it was great that Dad trusted me enough.

I still remember those sales, almost sixty years later. Because of the Coke. But also because I was important.

And for a kid, that's pretty cool.

Fishing

As I've said, I grew up around the water. We swam in the lake, took boat rides on the river, and we fished.

Fishing was just something we did. Growing up, I figured everybody fished. Because we did it quite often. When I was a little older, Dad bought a tiny boat, then another slightly bigger one. Neither were huge, but we'd go out fishing in them.

Today, Port Clinton is known as the walleye capital of the world. Or at least that's what we like to call it. No proof if it's true or not. But in my childhood, there were few walleye in the lake. At least I don't remember any. Part of the reason, I think, is because in the 60s, the lake was too polluted for them. It hadn't always been that way. My dad's family were commercial fisherman, and every day they took big ugly steel-gray boats out on the lake, cast their nets, and brought in fish. Perch, mostly. Dad used to say, "When we were out fishing, we'd pee off one side of the boat, and drink water from the other side." That might be somewhat of a tall tale, but maybe not. The lake had once been pretty clean. Luckily, due to a bunch of laws and other actions, Lake Erie is much cleaner than when I was a kid. Enough that the lake has a lot of walleye. Though I still don't think I'd want to drink right out of the lake.

But that's not my story here. My story is about when us kids went fishing on our own. We didn't drive, and were too young to take a boat. So we'd bike to the pier and fish there.

The pier was, and still is, a bunch of rocks piled in a long line that extends the mouth of the Portage River out into the lake. It's probably about 100 yards long. Today, it's pretty easy to walk on, as the rocks are mostly flat. But when I was a kid, they were just piled. There were no flat surfaces. So walking out on the pier carrying a fishing pole and a tackle box was tricky. I'm sure that if our moms realized how difficult it was, they wouldn't have let us do it. But we never fell in. Luckily.

We always used worms for bait, but we didn't buy them. I mean, who would buy worms? They were in our yard for free. When we were going to go fishing, we'd go into our yard the night before with a flashlight, hoping the ground was wet with dew. If not, we'd spray it with the hose and wait a while. Then, we'd walk slowly along, shining a flashlight on the grass. The earthworms (or nightcrawlers as they're sometimes called) would reflect the flashlight beam. If we were quick, we could grab them before they could go back into their hole. On a good night, we got plenty of worms. We'd put them in a container and put them in the fridge. I'm not sure why we refrigerated them, but the bait stores did, so we did. I'm sure Mom loved having worms in her fridge…

Normally, we didn't catch much. Even when we did, we never really knew what to do with them. Ideally, we'd clean them and have Mom fry them. But fish are not real easy to clean. When you get perch in a restaurant, you eat filets. All the bones had been removed. But as kids, we couldn't do that. The best we could do was to scrape all the scales off with a knife, cut off the heads and fins, and take out the guts. (I know that sounds gruesome. But the fish were dead by the time we did it. Promise!)

One time, I was fishing on the pier and I cast my line out, as we always did. Somehow I let go of the pole, and it flew out of my hand and went right into the river. Man, I was upset. It was my only fishing pole. (Yes, the fishing pole Jeff had bought me for my birthday.) I started crying. Of course. (Hey, I was a kid!)

But then a man who'd been fishing near us told me it would be alright. He said just give him a few minutes. He got in his car, and a few minutes later he was back, wearing a swimsuit. And honest to goodness, he jumped right into the Portage River to get my fishing pole.

Now, the Portage River is not a mountain stream. Its bottom is sand and mud, and it gets a lot of farm runoff. It's not exactly clean. Or clear. In other words, this good Samaritan was definitely swimming blind. He'd go under for a while, then come back up to get air. Then he'd do it again. It took a while, but eventually he came up with a triumphant, "Got it!"

Sure enough, my fishing pole was in his hand. And it still worked. I thanked the guy a zillion times, and he said it was no problem.

So it ended up being a good day. But I don't think we caught any fish.

Music Class

I remember fourth grade music class. We had art, music, and physical education, which were known as "specials." Once a week, the entire class went to specials for a half hour or so. And we'd learn music art, and phys ed.

Well, my favorite was music. I was never good at art, and phys ed was okay, but we got plenty of exercise on our own, so we didn't really have to have phys ed. Although I do remember learning how to square dance in phys ed, which honestly was kinda cool.

But music was the one for me. As I've said, we were a fairly musical family. We all could sing, or at least our church choir director told us so. Pat and Cathy were pretty good at the piano. By the time I was in fourth grade, they were both in the band and orchestra. Pat became first chair trombone, and Cathy was first chair trumpet. Yeah, we were pretty musical.

So I loved the class. I remember learning the difference between major and minor keys. We'd sing, a lot. And of course, we'd have programs once in a while that our parents came to. Sometimes we'd get simple instruments (sticks, triangle, drums, etc.). But mostly, we sang.

One day stands out in my mind. My class of probably about twenty-five was in the music room. The music teacher called a bunch of names, and told them to stand up. It was probably twelve or fifteen kids, a little more than half the class. I'm not sure exactly how many, but I know I was *not* asked to stand up.

Then the teacher said, "If you're standing up, you are one of the people I'm going to count on as our top singers."

Wait, what?

I was *not* one of the top singers? I just couldn't believe that. After all, we were a musical family. Maybe the teacher was right; maybe not. All I know is that I was really disappointed. I thought I was a good singer. But she apparently didn't think so.

Okay, to be fair, I might not have heard her correctly. In my adulthood, as a teacher, students remembered me saying things I definitely did *not* say. For instance, I was talking to one of my former students once. She was in her late twenties and said, "You know I'm a nurse now."

I replied, "That's great. Good for you."

She responded, "And I did it even though you told me I'd never make it. You told me I wasn't smart enough to be a nurse. But I worked hard, and I'm now a nurse. No matter what you told me, I made it. See, I *was* good enough."

Okay, it was great she was a nurse. And if she used my criticism as motivation, that's wonderful. But honestly, there is absolutely no way I would have said that to a student. Somehow, whatever I said, she heard it as *you're not smart enough.*

So maybe my fourth-grade music teacher didn't say it exactly as I remember it. Regardless, that's how I heard it, even if she didn't say it like that.

Later, when I was first-chair saxophone in the high school band, I remember thinking about my fourth-grade music teacher who didn't think I was good enough. Even now, I play the piano and sing, alone or in a band, quite a bit. In public. Sometimes they even pay me. So I guess I showed her!

Even if she didn't really say it the way I remember it.

Still, I remembered what (I thought) she said. Did it drive me to be a piano player and singer? I'm not sure. But I often think about that day, and how I proved her wrong.

I don't even remember that teacher's name. And most likely, she died some time ago. But I'd love to ask her about that, and see if I remember right.

And if it was as I remember, I'd feel completely justified in saying, "See, I *was* good enough!"

Why Are There Commercials?

In the 60s, television was nothing like it is today. With no cable and no streaming, most people used rabbit ears. This normally gave access to three channels: NBC, ABC, and CBS, all out of Toledo. Since Dad was in the business, we had a fifty-foot antenna tower, which brought in channels from Cleveland and Detroit as well—but still just the same three networks. Although in the summer when we were on daylight saving time, back then Cleveland wasn't. So we could watch certain shows early...or late. I could never get that straight.

I remember watching TV with Dad when a commercial came on. Being a kid, of course I complained: "Another commercial? Dad, why do we have to have commercials?"

Instead of blowing me off like parents do sometimes, he said, "Well, we pay for the TV, but we don't pay for the programs. And it costs a lot of money to make them. Instead of charging us for each show, they have commercials. The people who run them pay the TV stations."

That actually made sense. While I still didn't like commercials, at least I understood why. That was a bit of wisdom from my dad that I took to heart.

All that made sense at the time. But let's fast-forward about sixty years. Almost nobody does over-the-air TV anymore. We have cable, or streaming services, or if you're like me, both. I pay a lot for cable, and even more when you add in all the streaming services. And we *still* have commercials. In fact, we have lots more than we did sixty years ago. Go figure.

So Dad was right back in my childhood. But somehow the system changed, and we kept the commercials. I personally think Dad would be a bit upset about that today.

I know I am!

Sidewalk Sales

Like most small towns, we had a pretty decent downtown section. Back then, there were no huge stores, at least not in small towns. The downtown areas were usually full of retail stores that were really useful. And once a year, these stores had sidewalk sales.

Sidewalk sales, or "crazy day" sales, were exactly what they sound like. Retail stores displayed a bunch of their merchandise on the sidewalk in front of the store. These sales were near the end of summer. Since Port Clinton is a tourist destination in the summer, they were probably trying to get rid of the stuff that wasn't going to sell. Still, they seemed fun. I used to like to ride my bike down there and go all over town. I'd look at the toy stores and things like that. I was always sure I was going to get some great bargain.

One summer, I ended up at Green's Drug Store. In today's world of Walgreens, Walmart, and Rite-Aid, it's sometimes hard to imagine that small, independent stores like this existed. But they did, and we liked it.

Now, obviously at a young age I wasn't looking for pharmaceuticals. But like most stores, Green's sold other stuff. I remember looking at a display rack full of Port Clinton sweatshirts. There was one in particular that I thought was pretty cool.

It was white, with a Port Clinton stylized logo on the front, and it was just my size.

And it was a deal. It was marked at $2.89, but with a tag that said *1/3 off*. Okay, I was good at math; I could figure it out. I stood looking at this sweatshirt for quite a while, deciding if I should spring for it. That was a lot of money back then, and I've always been a little cheap. I never wanted to spend too much. So I did the math in my head. Then I did it again. And again. I must have stood there for twenty minutes, calculating, checking my money, and deciding if I should buy it.

Finally, I decided to go for it. I took the sweatshirt to the counter. I knew exactly what it was going to cost. When I handed it to the lady, I said, "It's just a little bit under a dollar."

Okay, for the mathematicians reading this, you've already picked up that I was, apparently, *not* as good at math as I thought. The woman said, "No, it's more than a dollar."

How could that be? I *knew* what 1/3 meant.

Then she said, "It's actually almost two dollars."

I was puzzled, upset, embarrassed, you name it. I was *sure* she was wrong. But as a kid, I didn't question adults. And I was too embarrassed to back out. So I paid the almost-two-dollars price, and took the sweatshirt away.

It was only then that I realized my problem. I'd read the tag as *Priced at 1/3*. Huge difference. So yes, I calculated the one third correctly. But that's not what it said. Because *1/3 off* means the cost is two thirds of the regular price, not one third. Stupid error. I was really mad at myself.

On the other hand, I really liked the sweatshirt. I wore it all the time. I don't remember if I ever told anyone about my math error. Probably not, because I was pretty embarrassed. But once the embarrassment ran its course, I decided it was really okay. After all, I actually had enough money to pay for it, it didn't break me, and I really liked the sweatshirt.

So I wore it. I loved it. I didn't get rid of it till it was way too small for me. And I forgave myself for the math error. I decided the sweatshirt was worth "almost two dollars" after all.

Sometimes, mistakes aren't so bad. It's a lesson I learned, but have to keep relearning it. I hate it when I make mistakes.

But ten-year-old me was okay with it. Because it allowed me to have my favorite sweatshirt.

Good Friday Easter Eggs

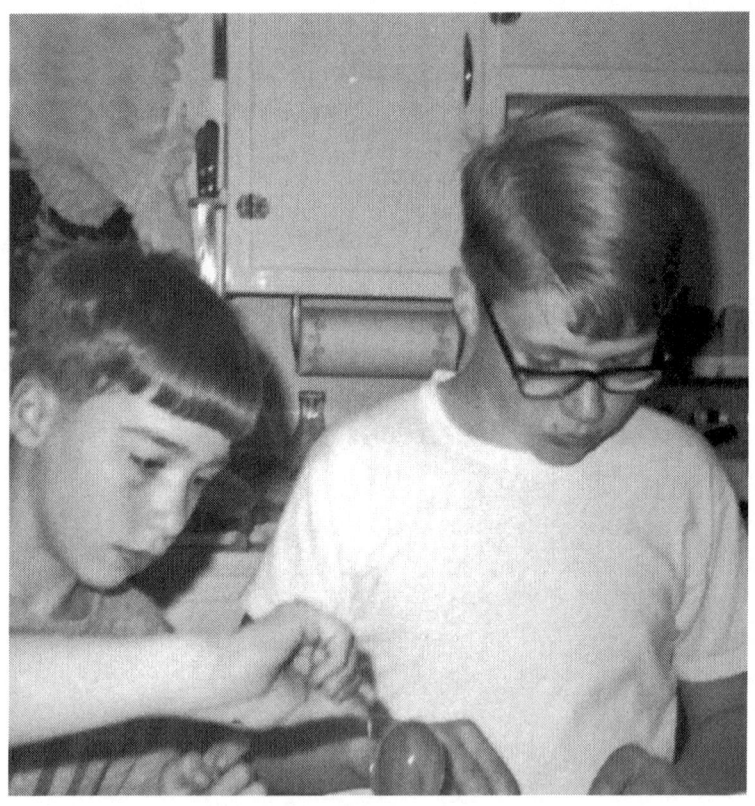

Dick and Jeff coloring Easter Eggs

    One family tradition I somehow remember distinctly was Easter with my grandparents.

    As I've said, Grandpa and Grandma Nitschke lived in Fremont. Since it was only a twenty-minute drive, we saw them quite often, and definitely every holiday and special occasion.

While of course Christmas and Thanksgiving were big deals, it's Easter that was amazing.

Easter at their house consisted of two parts. On Good Friday night, we went to their house to color eggs. I don't think Dad went, but Mom did, with us four kids. Our cousins lived farther away in Michigan, so while they came for Easter, coloring eggs was mostly a Morgan family affair. Although as I got older and it seemed pretty boring, I remember roping some of my friends into it as well.

First there was the coloring. We had to color enough eggs for all six grandchildren to hunt. So, what was the appropriate amount? Maybe six dozen, so each kid got about twelve eggs? Or go crazy and get twelve dozen eggs? That's two dozen eggs per kid. Most Easter baskets didn't hold that many.

Well, if you picked either of these, you'd be wrong. Grandma Marvel apparently really loved coloring eggs. Each year, we had a minimum of *twenty-two* dozen eggs. Sometimes much more. That's a *lot* of eggs.

It took forever. She just kept boiling eggs all night. She'd bring a batch to the kitchen table, and we'd set to work coloring them. Then she'd bring out another batch. We'd dye them as well. And she kept bringing out more, and more, and more...

You can probably see how that went. For the first batch, we were very careful. We'd write names on them, do multiple colors, and add stripes or fancy designs. That was great for a while. But twenty-two dozen is a lot of eggs. At some point, we realized it would take all night. When we started getting tired of eggs, we dumped them in any cup of dye we could find, and however it looked was how it looked. I always had one cup of purple dye, just for me. And I let an egg sit in there all night, to get the deepest purple egg possible.

A few of the eggs were designated as "onion skin" eggs. Grandma would boil them in, of course, onion skins, and they'd get this brownish color to them. Grandma and Mom liked them, but we were kids. We wanted brightly colored eggs. I mean, who wants a bunch of boring brown ones? If I remember right, they looked just like the brown eggs you can buy at the store. But Grandma thought they were cool, and we certainly had enough to color, so it was all good.

Regardless, by the end of the night, we had colored a zillion eggs. Grandma greased them with butter to make them shiny, and put them in the refrigerator. (I think she did, but really, I'm not sure how she fit twenty-two dozen eggs in her fridge, so I might be wrong on that part.)

We'd then go home and wait for Easter. The Easter weekend was just getting started.

Easter Morning Easter Eggs

Pat, Jeff, Cathy & Dick Morgan

All dressed up for Easter

Easter was a huge deal in our household. While we colored the eggs on Good Friday, Easter morning was, of course, the real holiday.

When we woke up, the first thing we'd notice was an Easter egg in one of our shoes. In fact, we'd leave a pair of shoes right by the bed for the Easter Bunny to fill. Kinda like

Christmas stockings I guess. Then we'd go downstairs and hunt eggs in the house. But we were just getting started. We'd eat breakfast, then go back upstairs and get into our best Sunday outfits. The girls had bonnets and dresses. Us boys had sport coats, and sometimes even fedoras. I remember Dad climbing up to a high shelf to get our hats, which we only wore on very special occasions. Then we'd all walk to Sunday school and church. *Then* we'd come back home, and when we were told it was okay, we'd hunt eggs outside.

You'd think that would be enough hunting. Not even close. We only had a small amount of eggs at our house. I don't know for sure, but I'm guessing we used some eggs from Friday.

Then we'd make the trip to Fremont. As we drove up, we could see a whole bunch of eggs "hidden" in the yard. When you have that many eggs, you run out of good hiding spots. I think Grandpa put them anywhere, sometimes just in the grass. Those weren't difficult to find.

But we weren't allowed to hunt them yet. Nope. First we had to go inside, where eggs were *everywhere*. Again, we couldn't hunt them right away. We had to wait for our cousins, Jeri and Jon, to get there. Once everyone was there, and when Grandpa was ready, we were allowed to start. First we hunted inside. We had to get all the inside ones before we were allowed to go outside. As soon as allowed, we'd run outside, because that's where most of the eggs were.

The funny thing is, it seemed to take forever. Yes, twenty-some dozen eggs take a while, but still it seemed to take much longer than necessary. I didn't know why until years later.

Because there were so many eggs, our Easter baskets got so full we couldn't carry them. (One time I tried, and unfortunately, I dropped the basket and broke a whole lot of eggs. Darn!) So we'd set our baskets down, then hunt more eggs and bring them back to the basket. What I didn't know was that Grandpa Clarence loved watching us kids hunt eggs. When we set our baskets down, he'd steal eggs out of them and hide them all over again. This explains why Grandpa always seemed to be giggling while we were hunting. And why it took so long.

Eventually, we'd get them all, even with Grandpa's cheating. And every year, no matter what happened, Jeff always had the most eggs. Every single time. He could find them in places I wouldn't even think to look. I think he ran faster too. All I know is that his basket was so full, we had to put all his eggs in grocery bags.

Of course, what does a mom do with that many eggs? Remember, these weren't plastic eggs filled with candy, like some people do now. They were real hard-boiled eggs. So Mom made egg salad for weeks. And creamed eggs on toast (I didn't like that very much) and every other egg dish she could think of.

I've never seen an Easter anywhere quite like the ones we had. Coloring twenty-two dozen eggs, (sometimes more) and hunting them as well? At the time, I didn't appreciate how much work it was for Grandma and Grandpa. Now that I'm older, I understand it was truly a labor of love. Nothing made them happier than seeing their grandkids happy. While we may not have been crazy about eating hard-boiled eggs, we sure loved hunting them. Which made them happy as well.

Sadly, of course, that tradition had to come to an end. I mean, kids grow up. I remember hunting eggs in high school! Because we were expected to. While I was a know-it-all teenager, I didn't really mind. By that time, Grandma and Grandpa were much older and not as healthy.

So Easter kinda turned around. When we were little, the grandparents made us happy by letting us hunt all those eggs. As we grew up and they aged, we made them happy by still doing it.

Eventually, when Grandma and Grandpa were unable to host, it moved to Mom and Dad's house. I was away at college for many of those, but for a few years at least, the tradition lived on. Instead of us four kids doing the coloring and hunting, it was the next generation of grandkids, which is somehow as it should be.

Eventually, my mom and dad got too old, and finally, the tradition ended. Yes, that's sad, but it's also life. All traditions die at some point. Which is okay. But still, the longer we keep them going, the better we feel.

And the more it allows us to honor the past. Which is definitely a good thing.

The Pinewood Derby

During elementary school, I was in Cub Scouts. I did it because I thought everybody did. My brother was in Cub Scouts. Davey was in Cub Scouts. Johnny was in Cub Scouts. So it only followed that I would be as well.

Once a week, we met in the Kallenbachs' basement. Mrs. Kallenbach and Mrs. Zekany were our den mothers. Looking back on it, it seems odd that a bunch of boys had den mothers. Not den fathers. I don't know if that was by design, or if it was because we met after school, and in the 60s, most mothers were home and most dads were at work. It would have been difficult for a man to run a Cub Scout den. In fact, I never knew of one den father. Only den mothers.

There were about eight or ten boys in our den. Once a month or so, we had a meeting of the pack. The pack was a much larger group, made up of probably eight or ten dens. There were lots of boys in the pack. And the pack leader was a man. Of course. It was the 60s, after all.

I really loved Cub Scouts. As you can imagine, we had all kinds of projects, mostly crafts. And we played lots of games. It was a good time. I really enjoyed hanging out with the other Cub Scouts. Oddly enough, I was assigned to a den with nobody I knew. Not Jeff, or Johnny, or anybody from my neighborhood. But that didn't matter. We all quickly became fast friends. Sixty years later, I'm still friends with Dick and Andy. In fact, when I got married a few years back, Dick was my best man!

I remember once, the entire pack had a project together: the Pinewood Derby.

The idea was pretty simple. Each boy received a Pinewood Derby kit that consisted of, if I remember correctly, a small block of wood, four wheels, and some other smaller parts. We were told to go home and, with the help of our dads, build a car out of this. There were rules about what we could use, how much it could weigh, and more. We were given about a month to work on this. Us kids, and our dads. At the end of that time, every kid in the pack would meet in a big room with two ramps. We'd race these cars down the ramps. It was like a tournament; if you beat the other car, you raced again. As long as you kept winning, you kept racing. There were prizes for the fastest few cars, as well as awards for creative designs and things like that.

The trouble was, my dad worked. All the time. And Mom either didn't or couldn't help me. So I built it by myself. (Which, honestly, was okay.) I sanded it (a little) and shaped it (kinda). But when I put the wheels on, it looked pretty much like what it was: a block of wood with four wheels.

A week or so before the big race night was a trial run. I took my car, disguised as a block of wood, to the practice. I couldn't believe what I saw. Every single car was way cooler than mine. Nobody else's looked like a block of wood. Most were painted; some had been formed into a completely different shape somehow. Some used "plastic wood" to modify it. Some put weights on it to make it go faster. There were a lot of really cool cars. Then there was...mine.

I was pretty embarrassed, but I ran through the trial race like I was supposed to. No, I didn't win. In fact, mine did horribly. I don't think I put it together quite right. But I looked at the other cars. I saw what they had done. And I vowed to make mine as cool and fast as theirs.

Armed with ideas, I worked pretty hard on it. I added some plastic wood to give it character. I sanded a lot to round out the edges. And I painted it. Plus a few other things. And my final product was...better. No, in no way could you say it was good, but it was better. I was ready for the race. Or, at least as ready as I could be.

The big night came. I took my (slightly) improved car to the school where the ramps were set up. When they called my name for my first run, I dutifully set my car at the start. Then they lifted the starting gate, which allowed both cars to start at the same time. My car took off...kinda. But it wasn't close. I lost, by a lot.

But it was okay. Really. I knew my car wasn't very good. It wasn't fast at all. And it didn't even look very cool. It looked like a car a less-than-talented eight-year-old would make.

Some cars there really were neat. Some had fashioned little toy men that looked like they were driving. Some added things that looked like tail pipes, or windows, or all kinds of other stuff that made the cars look cool. My friend Dick had a lot of help from his dad, and his dad had put some big nails on it, laying across the sides to give it extra weight. The judges thought the nails looked like some kind of exhaust pipes, and he got the award for most imaginative.

I kept a lot of things from my childhood, but I have no idea what became of my Pinewood Derby car. I'm guessing I threw it out because, let's face it, it didn't exactly "bring me joy." And that's okay. A lot of things from my childhood were very good experiences. But the Pinewood Derby was not one of those. Luckily, while I was in Cub Scouts for over three years, we only had one Pinewood Derby. If we had more, I've blotted them out of my mind.

Thankfully!

A Partridge in a Pear Tree

When I was a kid, our family always spent Christmas Eve at Grandma and Grandpa's in Fremont. They really, really went all out. We'd walk in the front door, and there would be literal mounds of presents. It was every kid's dream.

But of course, before we could open the presents, we had to make the twenty-minute drive. I remember one Christmas Eve drive vividly.

I'm not sure what time we were supposed to leave, but I know Dad was late. He had to work, of course, but his store should have been closed long ago, and he should have been home in plenty of time. Except he wasn't. Mom was *not* happy. Not at all.

Finally, he walked in and said, "Let's go. Pat, you're driving."

What? Pat had just turned sixteen a month before. She didn't have a driver's license, but she did have a permit that allowed her to drive when accompanied by a licensed driver. This was a bit extreme; she had hardly been behind the wheel. You wouldn't think her first big outing would be driving twenty minutes on a dark winter night with six people in the car.

Yet Dad said she was going to drive. And Mom was not pleased. I could tell that. But I didn't understand what was going on. Not until later.

We all piled in the car with Pat in the driver's seat and Dad in her seat in the back. What a hoot! Even today, I remember how scared Pat looked when she started driving. But that's not why I remember it. I remember it because Dad kept singing "The Twelve Days of Christmas." That was unusual, because Dad almost never sang. Also, he couldn't remember any of the words. All the way over to Fremont, he was trying to sing. But he had to keep stopping to say, "Okay, what comes next?"

Us kids knew the song, so we helped him out. I thought it was hilarious. We'd never had so much fun driving.

But Mom was still pissed.

As we were driving, even eleven-year old me could see Pat was not enjoying this. She was scared to death. She kept saying she didn't want to drive, and Dad kept saying, "You're doing fine." Then he sang some more. All the way to Fremont. It was only a twenty-minute drive, and Pat got us there safe and sound.

But Mom was still pissed.

Christmas Eve progressed as it normally did. A huge dinner, followed by presents, presents, and more presents. When it was time to leave, Dad got back in the driver's seat. But there was no singing this time.

What my eleven-year-old self didn't know, and didn't figure out till years later, was that Dad didn't drive because he was drunk. Apparently they had a party at work, and he drank…a bit too much. In Dad's later years, alcohol became somewhat of a problem for him. But back then, he didn't drink much. I had never seen him drunk. I'm pretty sure I didn't know for sure what "drunk" was. Probably the only exposure I had to it was Otis on *The Andy Griffith Show*.

In the end, we were all safe. And Dad did show some smarts by having Pat drive. I'll give him credit for not trying it himself. Why Mom didn't drive, I'm really not sure. But Dad said for Pat to drive, and she did.

While it ended up okay, I figured out one thing. I now know why Mom was pissed!

Camp Miakonda

After Cub Scouts was done, I became a Boy Scout. And it was great. We did all kinds of fun things: camping, hiking, and more. But the biggest event of the year, by far, was summer camp at Camp Miakonda.

Camp Miakonda (pronounced "may-a-KON-duh") was great. An entire week away from home, roughing it. It was a big deal. We'd arrive on Sunday afternoon and leave on Saturday morning. It wasn't just our troop; it was many, many troops. There were hundreds of scouts at any one time at Camp Miakonda. It was something we planned for, and anticipated, all year long.

This place was huge. Just a great big wooded area, hundreds of acres. It had a gigantic swimming pool, a lake, a huge mess hall, a trading post, and more. While maybe it wasn't exactly roughing it, it wasn't easy, either. There were no cabins for the scouts. There were three types of lodging. Tents slept two scouts. Tent cabins were eight-by-ten-foot structures with a wooden base and walls, and a tent for the roof. I think we fit four in there. Adirondacks, three-sided wood structures, slept four. With only three sides, that meant we had to deal with bugs and critters. But we were kids, and didn't really mind any of that.

We cooked some of our meals over the campfire, but for evening meals we always ate in the mess hall, a very big building with rows and rows of tables and hundreds of noisy kids. The water had a sulfur smell to it, and since our drinks in the mess hall were some kind of lemonade/Kool-Aid concoction, it stank. We called it "bug juice."

We were busy all week. We went to classes to earn merit badges. We went hiking on the trails, swimming in the pool, and canoeing on the lake. Wednesday night was parents' night. We had a big program, all of us scouts and our parents. While we sat as a troop, and not with our parents, we still got to talk to them before and after the program. For the kids who got homesick, that helped. But I never got homesick. It was all just fun.

One of the years we went there, it rained. Not just off and on, but constant. The entire week. We didn't see the sun till we went to the parking lot to leave on Saturday morning. Really. Everything was soggy and muddy. All week.

That year, I had signed up for cooking merit badge. To earn it, I went to three or four classes during the week where an instructor taught us how to start a fire, how to cook certain things, and all the safety requirements we needed to know. The last day of the class, we had our test. We had to start a fire using only two matches, and make and cook our meal.

Since it had rained all week, there was no chance of finding any dry wood to use as kindling for the fire. This is where John comes in. John was our Scoutmaster. I don't remember too much about him, except that we was very good to all of us, treated us well, and behaved exactly like you'd want a

Scoutmaster to behave. While it doesn't have any effect on this story, I remember he drove a Corvair, which we all thought was pretty cool.

Also, John was honest. He made a point of teaching us about honesty and integrity. Like I said, he was excellent. But John was really worried about me starting this fire. So he did a very "un-John" thing. Before I went to the cooking test, he soaked some small twigs in lighter fluid, just in case. He explained that he wouldn't normally do that, but since these were extreme circumstances, he felt justified. Still, I know he didn't really like it.

He went with me to the test, and watched as I built the fire. Amazingly, I got it going without the illegal kindling. He and I were both relieved. I could tell he wasn't comfortable with "cheating," so he was glad when I didn't need them. I don't remember the main dish, but I know we made a baked apple with butter, cinnamon, and sugar. And we also cooked a biscuit. I have no idea what I used to make this biscuit. But to this day, I have never had a better baked apple or biscuit. They were that good. At least in my mind. Needless to say, I passed, and earned my cooking merit badge.

One time, my friend Bob (the same Bob who we hunted snakes with) and I had some free time, and we were exploring the huge camp. We were careful about getting lost, because it was gigantic, and we were in the middle of nowhere. During our exploration, we came to a chain-link fence that marked the camp boundary. On the other side of the fence was a golf course. A golf course? We didn't understand, because we were in the middle of nowhere. Yet, there it was.

It wasn't till years later when I was an adult, driving through Toledo, that I happened to see the entrance to Camp Miakonda. It wasn't remote at all. It was, and still is, right in Toledo. We always felt like we were miles away from civilization, yet all the time we were in a city.

I think it's a testament to Camp Miakonda and its staff that we always felt like we were far away from civilization. That's what summer camp is supposed to be like, and that's exactly what it felt like.

So no, I wasn't in the wilderness. But for all we knew, we might as well have been. A week camping in the wilderness, complete with all the bugs and animals you'd expect.

As a kid, I couldn't ask for much more.

Of Batteries and Bulbs

During my childhood, there were no remote-controlled (RC) cars. Or RC planes. Or really RC anything. We always thought it would be really cool. But in the 60s, that didn't exist. Or if it did, it was so far out of our price range that we didn't know anything about it.

But I *did* have a model helicopter that actually flew. Well, it "flew" with a little imagination. It wasn't radio controlled, of course. Instead it was attached to a very light rod, about six feet long. You put batteries in the helicopter and turned it on, and the rotors would start up. Then, basically, you just twirled it around and around over your head. It wasn't particularly realistic, but that wasn't all bad. Because I got to imagine anything I wanted to.

Yes, in today's world, that sounds pretty uncool. I guarantee that if you gave something like that to a young child now, that kid would *not* be pleased. Not in these times. And honestly, I wouldn't blame him. There are so many better options now. I mean, compare my helicopter to a drone you can buy pretty cheap today. My helicopter would definitely be uncool.

But as I've said so many times, the world was different back then. In that world, the helicopter was actually pretty cool. The other thing was, it took a whole lot of imagination to make it fun. When I was in the backyard twirling it round and round,

OF BATTERIES AND BULBS

I had to imagine the stories behind it. Was I out sightseeing? Or was I in a rescue? Or was I in battle? Because that chopper wasn't high in realism, it required imagination to make it fun. That's not really a bad thing.

As you can imagine, one day, it stopped working. The batteries were dead. Of course it didn't stop all at once. As the batteries were dying, the rotors turned slower and slower, till finally it didn't work at all. I told Dad, and he put a couple new batteries in the toy, and all was good. There were no rechargeables back then.

One day, I was using a flashlight for something. It kept getting dimmer and dimmer. You'd think I'd have known it needed new batteries. But I was either stupider than most or smarter than most. You can decide. I looked at this problem like my helicopter. Except a flashlight is different in that it has *two* parts that can fail: the batteries and the bulb.

I remembered that once Mom had replaced a flashlight bulb when it didn't work. And it was fixed. I didn't know if I had to replace the batteries or the bulb, so I asked Dad.

He said, "It can't be the bulb. Bulbs don't run down. They either work, or they don't."

Who knew? Well, I know now. Looking back, I should have figured it out. But I didn't. Dad once again replaced the batteries, and all was well.

I think the reason I remember this seemingly insignificant story is because I learned something. I didn't know, really, the difference between batteries and bulbs. I just knew you needed both of them for the flashlight to work. But once Dad told me that, and gave me a little bit of background on how a flashlight works, filaments and all that, it all made sense. Although it was a little thing, I learned something about everyday objects, batteries and bulbs, that I hadn't known. I liked that Dad made a point of taking enough time to explain it to me, to teach me. I always liked it when that happened. It didn't happen all that often. Dad was always working, and when he got home, as you can imagine, he was always tired. He didn't always take a lot of time to teach us things. So when he did, it was pretty special.

Dad taught me about batteries, and now I know. A simple lesson, but one I appreciated.

I Got You Last

One time, we were visiting Grandma and Grandpa Nitschke in Fremont. I don't know what the occasion was. When we got ready to leave, Grandpa was watching us get in the car and was saying his good-byes. Right at that time, my sister Pat got out of the car, ran up to Grandpa, tapped his shoulder, and said, "I got you last!"

What? What's going on? I had no idea, but Grandpa started chuckling. When we were all in the car, he went to Pat's window to say goodbye and quickly tapped Pat on the shoulder, saying, "I got you last."

Pat giggled and tried to tap him back. I don't know who "won" that round, but it became a thing. Whenever we were leaving their house, or when they were leaving ours, Pat and Grandpa would get into a "tapping" war. It must have been fun, because they were both always giggling. This went on for years. They did it every time they saw each other.

Grandpa always wore a hat. If he was going someplace nice, he wore a fedora. But mostly, he wore a baseball hat. Back in those days, most baseball hats didn't have logos on them. Unless, of course, you were on a baseball team. Mostly, they were just boring, solid colors. And Grandpa used to wear a gray one. Either way, he always wore some kind of hat.

Grandpa was also a homebody. If he was visiting, way before we thought they should leave, he'd say "It's time to go." So we used to steal his hat and hide it. That way he couldn't leave. He was always a good sport about it, and always found it. But we liked keeping him here.

I have three modern-day takeaways about this.

One: as an adult, I'm also a homebody. Whenever I'm away, even if I'm enjoying myself, I look forward to being home. I like to think I inherited that from Grandpa.

Two: I wear baseball hats all the time now. I almost always wear a boring gray one, just like Grandpa. Partly because I really like gray. But also to honor Grandpa Clarence.

Three: Finally, years later, I asked my sister why she did the "I got you last" thing. She told me (and this is *so* Pat) that one time we were leaving and Grandpa looked sad. To make him feel better, she ran to him and said "I got you last." She did it because she thought he was feeling left out. And it worked. Grandpa probably knew why she was doing it, but even if he did, he certainly didn't care. His granddaughter was trying to make him happy.

And how can you not be happy with that?

Fifth Grade School Birthday Party

In elementary school, it was common for kids to bring treats in for their birthdays. Somehow I doubt that's much of a thing anymore. I mean, do I really want to eat food that came from some random kitchen, made by some random person I know nothing about? Also, lots of kids have dietary restrictions they didn't have sixty years ago.

But back then, it was common. Since my birthday is in September, I was always one of the first to bring something in. Normally it was cupcakes or brownies, or something like that. But I remember very vividly that this time, I brought Hershey bars. Full-size ones, of course. I have no idea why it wasn't baked goods; for some reason, I chose Hershey bars. All candy bars were a nickel, unless you got one of the huge ones they sold at the grocery store. But we always bought regular size. Honestly, I'm not sure "fun size" was even a thing.

The trouble was that I knew one of my classmates, Donna, was diabetic. I didn't know exactly what that meant, but Mom explained to me that she might not be allowed to eat the candy bar. But I didn't want to leave Donna out. I thought if I gave her something completely different, that might draw attention to her. Even if I could have figured out what substitute treat was fitting.

I came up with the perfect solution. At least I thought it was. I can't believe Mom let me do this, but hey, it was my birthday I guess. My solution? As I walked around the class handing each kid a candy bar, when I got to Donna's desk, instead of the candy bar, I handed her a nickel. It seemed fair to me; the Hershey bar cost a nickel, and I didn't want to cheat her, so I figured with the nickel she could buy whatever treat she wanted.

Looking back on it, it probably wasn't the best solution. But in my ten-year-old brain, it was perfect.

I never asked Donna what she thought—until recently. As Donna still lives in the area, I see her occasionally. But it wasn't until our fiftieth class reunion that I asked her about this. And believe it or not, she actually remembered. And she seemed just fine with it.

So maybe it was the right decision after all.

The Jump That Wasn't

Second place trophy, a bit late

Back in elementary school, some group in my hometown decided to have a junior Olympics. They planned a track meet for elementary kids. We could all enter, for free, and compete in sprints, jumps, runs, etc. And if we did well enough, we'd get ribbons.

Ribbons? That would be cool.

Well, I knew I was pretty fast. Not as fast as my friend Johnny, but faster than a lot of the other neighborhood kids. Accounting for age anyway, since I was the youngest. But I knew I was fast, and I could jump. So Mom and Dad signed me up for the long jump and the fifty-yard dash.

I was pretty excited. I knew I could win a ribbon. I had never won any kind of award before, so I was looking forward to it.

I think the whole family went. Which was unusual. Honestly, I don't remember if my sisters went, but I know Jeff did, as well as Mom and Dad. Dad? Well, that was something. Dad was normally busy working, so he didn't go to a lot of these things. But he went to this one.

And who else was there? Jesse Owens. Yes, that Jesse Owens. The Jesse Owens who won four Olympic gold medals in the 1936 Berlin Olympics. The guy Hitler was angry about because Owens was Black. That didn't fit with Hitler's Aryan supremacy ideas.

At the track meet, someone asked Owens how far he could jump when he was young. He answered, "About five feet farther than this pit." I guess that was funny, because everybody laughed.

I really do wish I had known more about Jesse Owens at the time. Instead of meeting some unknown famous guy, it would have meant a lot more. But this story isn't really about Jesse Owens; it's about the track meet.

My first event was the fifty-yard dash, and I didn't win. I wasn't even close. I remember Joe Lymon won. Joe Lymon? We didn't know he was fast. Yet, he was. I got fifth. Not great, and not good enough for a ribbon, but fifth out of a lot was pretty good. I was happy.

I couldn't wait for the long jump. I just knew I could win a ribbon.

At the long jump area, they told us the rules: go to the opposite end of the runway, run as fast as we could, and when we got to the takeoff board, jump as far as we could. If our foot went over the board, it would be a foul and wouldn't count. We all got three jumps, so they explained that a foul didn't really hurt us, as long as we got in one good jump.

When it came time for me to jump, I did what they told me. I ran as fast as I could, then jumped. And I heard them yell, "Foul!"

Darn! That was no good. But I knew I had two more chances. And my next two jumps were better. I didn't foul on either. My best jump was 9' 9½". (Yes, I still remember.)

I was pretty stoked, because that was better than Johnny by half an inch. He jumped only 9' 9". Johnny was one of the best athletes in our class, and I was better than him. That had to be good. Right?

Soon, they announced the long jump results over the stadium speakers. They started at sixth place and worked up.

When they got to second place, they said, "In second place is Johnny Williams, with a jump of 9' 9"."

I was so excited, because that meant I'd won. I had to. Because I was better than Johnny.

But when they announced the winner, it wasn't me.

How could that be? I had jumped farther. I should have won. Or maybe I should've gotten second, and Johnny third. All I knew was, I didn't get a ribbon. I was absolutely crushed.

My parents really felt bad for me. I remember Mom saying that maybe it was because I had a foul. But I explained to her that they'd said it wouldn't matter.

Then Dad did something he didn't often do. He said, "I'll take care of it." And he went to the press box and talked to them.

I knew he'd fix it. But when he came back, he said that according to them, I didn't have the jump I thought I had.

I'll never know what really happened. I could have misheard my distance, but I don't think so. I'm pretty sure I was right. I was listening very carefully, and I understood fractions well enough to know my jump was better than Johnny's. Maybe it was written wrong. That's probably the most likely. I'm pretty sure the workers were high school kids from the track team, and I've worked enough track meets in my life to know it's easy to write something wrong, or miss a jump. Or something. It happens. Even in high school meets with registered officials.

Regardless, when the day was done, we walked home. I didn't cry, but I was decimated. While my family felt bad for me, there wasn't anything they could do. I didn't win a ribbon.

Then another thing happened. A little thing, but I still remember it. When we got home, my brother said, "Do you want a 7-Up?" We didn't have pop often, and it definitely wasn't something us kids gave each other. But even at that young age, and even in my sadness, I knew Jeff was doing all he could to make me feel better.

I accepted the 7-Up.

No, I didn't win. But as is often the case, some good came of it. Over thirty years later, when I was a track coach, I told a couple of my athletes this story. When the end of the year came and we had our awards ceremony, those athletes presented me with a trophy that said *1963, Second Place, Long Jump*. No, it wasn't the same as the ribbon I should've won. But it was gratifying that they cared enough to make sure I got the trophy. Even if it took thirty-some years.

The other good that came of it? I still remember how much my family tried to help me. Mom trying to come up with a reason. Dad trying to fix it. And Jeff pouring me the 7-Up.

So I didn't win. But really, if I had, I'm not sure I'd still remember it.

To be truthful, the memories of my family caring for me are better than a ribbon any day.

The Rifle Matches

Just a few miles from my hometown is Camp Perry. Back then, and still today, each summer it's the home of the National Rifle Matches. Along with that, at least in the 1960s, they had what they called the Instructor Junior School, which gave kids the chance to learn how to shoot from people who knew what they were doing. If I remember right, it was free. Even better!

The problem was that the minimum age was twelve. But I wanted to go when I was ten. Mom told me I was too young. So we compromised. She filled out the application, but she didn't lie. (Mom was honest to the extreme.) She put my age down exactly as it was: I was ten, with a birthday in a month.

And they accepted me. Yay!

I think I went for three years. The first year, we shot BB guns. We were only fifteen feet from the targets, because BB guns aren't particularly accurate. These BB guns were air powered, so while dangerous, they weren't lethal. The instructors taught us all the rules good gun owners should follow. No, none of us probably would have been seriously hurt with a BB gun, but they treated the guns as if they could kill us. Looking back on it, it was definitely the right thing to do. We learned to be careful, and respect the weapon.

The second year, we shot pellet guns. Air powered like the BB guns, they were a bit more powerful, so the targets were twenty-five feet away. By my second year, I found out I was a good shot. Not the best out there, but close.

The third year, we shot real .22 rifles and we were fifty feet from the target. I was still one of the best there. That year, my friend Dick was with me. I remember the instructor telling him that maybe he should just try to shoot elephants. No, he didn't really mean that. He meant Dick wasn't a very good shot, so he'd need a big target.

These were such fun times.

First of all, we were gone all day, all week actually, away from home and our parents. It made us feel very grown up. Besides that, we found the challenge of shooting a lot of fun. And I've always liked learning new things. So learning to shoot was a lot of fun.

Then there was the mess hall. They gave us an hour for lunch I think. And we were allowed to eat in the mess hall. Back then, Camp Perry was an active US Army base. So of course there was a mess hall. Not only did we get to eat as much as we wanted; we were with the soldiers. That was really neat as well.

(As an aside, my mom told me that one time she was at Camp Perry for some reason with my sister Cathy. At that time, Cathy was probably in high school. She was tall, blonde, and pretty. At one point a group of soldiers marched by, and the drill sergeant calling the cadence went from "Hup, two, three, four" to "Eyes left, two, three, four." Cathy, of course, was on the left, and the reason for the call. Somehow I don't think that would happen today!)

Another fun thing: on the final day, we only shot in the morning. There was a ceremony later in the day, so we had about three hours to kill on our own. And back then, there were a lot of commercial establishments on the base. I don't know if they were permanent, or just there for the National Matches. But it didn't matter, because it seemed like every store gave out free goodies. So whether we needed them or not, we got them. Free stuff is always good to a kid.

I don't shoot anymore, although I've thought about it a lot. Camp Perry is still there, and at certain times of the year they offer marksmanship classes. I've often thought about it. It could be fun. Although I'm guessing I'm not as good a shot as I once was.

And I'm not sure I'd like it as much as I did then. I was a kid doing something "adult," and that may have colored my thinking.

All I know is that I couldn't wait to go to the Rifle Matches each year.

The Charcoal Grill

I must have been about ten or eleven. Mom and Dad had a charcoal grill. Almost every family had one. Nobody had propane grills back then. Or wood-pellet fired. Or anything like that. We had charcoal.

One day, Mom wanted to grill out, and she found that our grill was unusable. It had rusted out completely. She was pretty upset, because she had dinner all planned.

Mom saw an ad in the paper that a charcoal grill was for sale for eight dollars at the local hardware store. She figured she could run down to the store, buy it, and have it assembled in time for supper. But she didn't have the cash on her. No, we weren't poor. (Or rich for that matter.) Whether she was between paychecks or just short of cash, I have no idea. All I know is that she couldn't buy the grill. She didn't have a credit card.

I said, "Mom, I have eight dollars from my paper route. Do you want to borrow it?"

She did. She thanked me properly, and she paid it back within a day or so.

I don't think she ever realized how cool that was. Buying a charcoal grill was a very adult thing to do. I secretly strutted around for a few days, thinking how adult and cool I was.

Sometimes it's the little things that make a difference in a kid's life. This was one of those.

Rockets

In fifth grade, I met Jim Hester. I was kinda a science nerd, but I was nothing compared to him. While I thought astronomy was cool, that was about as far as it went. He read science books. And magazines. All sorts of things like that. What made it really cool was that he liked rockets. Not only did he like them; he built them. And launched them.

Jim introduced me to model rocketry. It was so neat. The only company we bought from was Estes Industries. It still exists, and they still sell rockets.

Really, there was nothing cooler than getting the Estes catalog in the mail. They didn't sell their stuff in stores, and of course online wasn't a thing back then. So when we got the new catalog, it was a big deal.

These weren't like model airplanes. No, these were real rockets. That really flew. And they flew so high that a lot of times you couldn't even see them. And sometimes you lost them! They were made from cardboard and balsa wood mostly, and they were great.

When that catalog came, I'd pore through it. I didn't have a lot of money, just what I made from my paper route. So I had to pick and choose. Of course, I wanted the really tall, sleek ones that used a parachute for recovery. But those were

ROCKETS

pretty expensive, so I didn't often get ones like that. I bought the smaller, less expensive ones.

My first one was called the Sprite. It was only about six inches tall with a ring on the tail fins, and it had what was called tumble recovery. That meant that while it was falling back to earth, it would tumble end over end so it didn't fall very fast, preventing it from breaking when it hit the ground. Assuming it didn't land on concrete, or a roof, or something.

Launching them was only part of the fun. There was also the anticipation, which was frustrating, yet worthwhile. It took a week or two to go through the catalog over and over, narrow our choices to just a few rockets, then finally decide which one(s) to order. Plus we had to make sure we had all the accessories: launch system, engines, extra parts in case of breakage, and things like that.

There was no two-day delivery. We couldn't order online of course, or even by phone. We had to tear the order form from the catalog and fill it in by hand, hoping they could read our writing. Then we had to have Mom write a check, or go to the drug store and buy a money order.

And then we'd wait. If I remember right, it took three or four weeks. I'd check the mail every single day. There was, of course, no tracking information. So we'd check the mail. Every day. The anticipation was horrible. And wonderful. At the same time. On one hand, we wanted our order so bad. But on the other hand, the longer it took, the more excited we got.

Well, eventually of course, the package would come. But that was just the beginning. Remember, these were models; we had to put them together with X-ACTO knives, glue, paint, and more. Depending on the difficulty, it might take three days or three weeks.

But sooner or later, the rockets were ready to launch. We launched ours at the elementary school because there was a huge grass field behind it. We had to wait for a day with very little wind. Since they flew so high, it was easy to lose them. Which, of course, was very upsetting.

To launch them, we'd put them on the launch pad. That consisted of a metal plate so we didn't burn the grass, and a three-foot steel rod that guided the rocket in the first few feet. The engines were cardboard tubes that used gunpowder as a propellant, so it was a bit tricky. We were supposed to light them with an electrical igniter hooked to a car battery. Sometimes we did, but that meant we had to have a car, and normally our parents weren't with us. So sometimes we used Jet-X Wick, which was kinda like a firecracker wick. It wasn't as safe, but it worked. We'd light it and run eight or ten feet away.

When they launched, it was fast. Honestly, they are pretty amazing. If you've never seen one of these take off, well, you should. They're very impressive. If all went well, we'd be able to follow it as it shot up, then coasted for a while, then fell back to earth. We'd chase it, replace the engine, and launch it all over again—assuming it wasn't broken, and assuming we could find it.

ROCKETS

A number of times, a rocket ended up in a tree. Sometimes they took off so fast and went so high, we never even saw them. Sometimes, especially if a rocket used a parachute, it would blow away. We'd chase it on our bikes, and sometimes we'd find it. But sometimes it was just gone. Bummer, to be sure.

For me, the hobby went in spurts. I'd build and launch a few rockets, then I'd kinda ignore it for a few months, or even a few years, then do it all over again.

Gotta be honest, as an adult, I still periodically get the Estes bug. The cycle of searching the catalog (paper or online), making the order, waiting for delivery, assembly, and launch remains the same. Although we don't have to wait a month for our order to arrive anymore. (You can even buy some of them at Walmart now.) And the launch systems are better, so we don't use the wick. But we still fly them and lose them. Just like in the old days!

Of course, they cost much more than they used to. But I have more income sources than just a paper route, so it all works out.

To this day, there's something magical about launching rockets. Whether it's the throwback to my childhood, or just the wonder of watching something go so fast and so high, I'm not sure.

But I still get excited when my Estes catalog comes in the mail!

Age 11

My Best Bike

By about sixth grade, I was ready for a new bike. This one would be on me. But I knew what I was going to do. The year before, Jeff had bought a bike from MJ's bicycle shop on Third Street. A woman whose real name was Mary Jane sold Schwinn bikes out of her basement. And the cool thing was, she let Jeff pay on credit. Really. Jeff bought the bike, and the deal was he'd pay her two dollars per week until the bike was paid off. What a great service MJ gave him. I have no idea if that was common, or if it was because she knew our family. Or because he had a paper route. All I know is she did it.

When I was ready for a bike, I went to MJ. Right about that time, Schwinn came out with their Sting-Ray. The Sting-Ray was *not* your typical bike. Instead of being a twenty-six-inch bike like most "old kid" bikes, this was only twenty inches, so it was a little bike. But it was nothing like the little green bike I had when I was younger. No, the Sting-Ray defined cool. Banana seats, a gear shift on the bar, and weird over-your-head handlebars. I thought about it for a long time. Finally, I decided I wanted a regular bike. Or maybe I just didn't think I was cool enough for a Sting-Ray! My friend Andy had one, and he loved it. But Andy was always a little cooler than me.

I bought a beautiful gold Schwinn Typhoon. Without even asking, I told MJ I'd pay her two dollars per week, just like my brother. And she was fine with that. So I picked up the bike, and each week after I collected from my paper route, I rode to MJ's to pay my two dollars. I never once missed a payment.

It wasn't till a little bit later that Mom said, "You know, she doesn't have to accept payments like that. She can ask for all the money up front. She's doing you a favor."

I hadn't realized that. But it made sense. Maybe that's why I never missed a payment.

While I loved the bike, I did have a bit of buyer's remorse just a few weeks after I bought it. Because I saw Jake Smith ride by on a Schwinn bike that was almost identical. Same color and everything, except it was a *five speed*. I didn't care so much about the speeds, but that bike was just cooler. I remember Jake riding by, sitting up high, much higher than my bike. And it just looked cool. I told Dad, "I want to trade my bike in on a five-speed."

He said, "That's not really how it works. MJ can't sell your bike as new anymore. Would you want to pay for a new bike that's been ridden for a few weeks? Of course not."

That was my first lesson in depreciation. While Dad understood my thinking, I also understood what he said. And of course, MJ was being nice by extending credit, so I couldn't really blame her. Somehow, after a week or so, I forgot about Jake's bike, and was completely happy with mine.

There are a couple lessons there, and I think I absorbed both of them.

I rode that bike everywhere. It was part of me. I do remember, though, just after I bought it, a church youth group I was in was going on a bike trip. It would take a few hours and we'd ride quite a distance. But Pastor Luoma was going along, and he didn't have a bike. I told him I had *two* bikes, and he could use one of mine. He was very grateful, and accepted the offer.

So here was my conundrum: I had just recently purchased my new bike. So of course I wanted to ride that one on the bike trip. But I also knew that if I was really being decent, I'd lend Pastor the *new* bike, while I used the old one for that trip.

Gotta admit, I thought about that for a long time. But in the end, I did the right thing and lent Pastor the new bike. He was very grateful, and I really didn't mind riding my old one. I think that was probably another lesson of some kind I learned there as well.

I still have that Schwinn Typhoon. It's in my garage, along with a whole bunch of junk. Every year I say I'm going to restore it. But I never do. First I said I'd do it in my retirement. Well, I'm retired, and the bike still sits in a heap in a corner of the garage. Although I'm retired, I have a bunch of part-time jobs. Now I'm telling myself that when I re-retire, I'll fix that bike.

Realistically, as cool as that would be, I'll probably never restore it, no matter my intentions. But we'll see. I might die with that bike still sitting as is in a corner of my garage!

Maybe I'll restore it; maybe not. But I sure loved that bike.

Sixth Grade

Like everyone else, I've had good periods in my life, as well as some not-so-good. We all have highs and lows. I'm an old(er) man now, so you'd expect me to say my best years are somewhere behind me. While I really enjoy the age I am now, I have to say that yeah, my best years might be behind me. Although I hope not.

Specifically, I think my best year was sixth grade. Really. I peaked in sixth grade.

Why sixth grade? I mean, I was only eleven. What great things could have happened?

Well, first there were girls. I was noticing girls by then. No, I didn't really get the picture. But I knew girls were different. And I noticed.

But more importantly, they noticed me. Girls thought I was cute. And they liked me. I was popular with them. I have no idea why. While I've had a pretty good life all in all, in some ways, it's all gone downhill from there. (Okay, probably not. But it makes for a better story!)

Yeah, I may be exaggerating just a bit. But sixth grade was pretty cool. A big part of it was girls paying a lot of attention to me. But one other thing happened that I will never forget.

As I've said, in second grade, I was a good speller. Really good. Today, not so much. In fact, I'm pretty pathetic at it. I have no idea how that skill abandoned me. Yet, it is what it is.

Yes, I had been a great speller in second grade, but that was then. I was in sixth grade now, and that was much different. I had Mrs. Hess as a teacher, and she was great. We had a lot of fun. But most of my best and smartest friends from fifth grade were in Mrs. Borman's class.

One day, Mrs. Hess told us we were going to have a spelldown against Mrs. Borman's class. Well, that was cool. All the smartest kids were in Mrs. Borman's class, so it would be a challenge. We knew we didn't have much of a chance, but still, we were pretty stoked about it. We were definitely going to do our best.

When the big day came, all of us marched on down to Mrs. Borman's class. Why she got home field advantage, I have no idea. I didn't care. (I probably didn't even know what home field advantage was.) We lined up in two rows: us on one side of the room, and Mrs. Borman's kids on the other.

Let the battle begin.

It went pretty quickly at first. Some kids couldn't spell to save their lives, and they went down right away. (Honestly, looking back on it, I wonder how they felt. But that's a different subject.) I remember watching my classmates go down. Fast. Pretty soon there were eleven of the other class to just two of us. It was me and Jim Hester, the rocket guy, against all of them. It didn't look good.

But Jim was real smart. I mean he was a rocket/space geek; he *had* to be smart. And the other team started dropping. Soon it was us against ten, then nine, then eight. Now remember, we went back and forth between classes, so Jim and I had to spell a *lot* of words. With seven of them left, Jeff went down on *gantry*, the steel structure next to a rocket on the launchpad. How could he go down on that word? He was a rocket geek! But he did. It didn't look good. Not at all.

I was in trouble. There were seven of them against me, which meant I had to spell every other word. But I kept getting them right. Soon there were six of them, then five, then four. Now, all my classmates were cheering me on. And not quietly. It was as rowdy as any football game I've ever been to. We wanted to win.

Finally, it came down to me against their best speller. We went back and forth for the longest time, both getting all the words right. All the classmates were cheering like crazy every time we got one right. It was exciting. And tense.

Then, finally, it happened: my opponent missed a word. All I had to do was spell one more, and we'd be the champions. I don't remember the word, but I spelled it right. Woo Hoo!

We were the champions. We had won it. I had faced down the last seven all by myself and come out on top. My classmates went wild. Cheering and screaming, with one of my classmates, Fidel, cheering in Spanish! They were clapping, whooping, and celebrating every way a sixth grade kid knows how. It was like we had won the national championship.

And then it got even better. Before I realized what was happening, my classmates lifted me up on their shoulders and, cheering all the way, carried me back to our classroom.

I was a hero.

Was that really my peak? Of course not. But that was the only time in my life I had a team carry me on their shoulders. And it was pretty cool.

I've had a lot of successes since then. But that's right up there in my great moments.

So yeah, sixth grade was pretty cool.

Last Day for Lunch

When I was in elementary school, I loved walking to school. (No, it wasn't five miles, or uphill both ways.) It was only a few blocks. I was always glad I didn't have to take the bus. I'm not sure how many first graders walk to school today. I'm guessing it's very few, if for no other reason than neighborhood elementary schools are far less common than they used to be. But in the 60s, all the kids who lived close walked or biked to school. Well, at least everybody I knew.

One advantage of that was that we could go home for lunch. I almost never ate in the school cafeteria, unless they had fish sticks or apple crisp. Those were my favorites!

Once we were in junior high, we had a closed lunch. We couldn't go home, but instead had to eat in the cafeteria.

Back then, junior high started in seventh grade. Grades one through six were at the elementary. The last day of sixth grade was the last day I ever went home from school for lunch.

Of course, if I went home for lunch, someone had to be there to feed me. I didn't do a lot of cooking in sixth grade! Mom was always there. She didn't cook fancy stuff, but it was always okay with me. One common meal was little tiny pizzas, probably about five inches across. I'm pretty sure the brand was GW, which I'm sure doesn't exist anymore. Alas.

I actually remember the last day I was home, because of what happened. I was sitting at the counter eating my pizza, and Mom was in the kitchen, probably cleaning up. Knowing it was my last day home, I said to her, "Mom, do you know that today is the last day any of your kids will come home for lunch?"

Now, to an eleven-year-old, that sounds like a pretty harmless statement. I didn't mean anything by it. But to a mom, it was more than that. When I said it, she looked at me, paused, and then started crying.

At first, I couldn't figure it out. But very quickly I realized: she was sad, as all parents are, when their kids pass some stage in their lives. It means an era has gone. And when the *last* kid passes that stage, it's especially hard. As a father, I now completely understand. Mom wasn't mad at me; she understood. She was just sad. In some ways, it was a good sad, but still sad.

Like I said, I was eleven and didn't know better. But a little over six years later, I was heading off to college. Once again, I said, "Mom, do you realize that today is the last day any of your kids will head off to college?"

This time I really should have known better. I wasn't being mean. But also, I wasn't thinking. Once again, Mom looked at me, paused, and started crying.

That time, I really did feel bad. Becoming an empty-nester makes life easier. But it sure makes life more lonely. Mom was looking back at all those twenty-three years, most of her adult life, when she had kids at home, and now that part of her life was behind her. That's a hard thing for any parent to face. No wonder she cried.

I really, really should've known better. Mom got over it of course, but I feel bad about it.

To this very day.

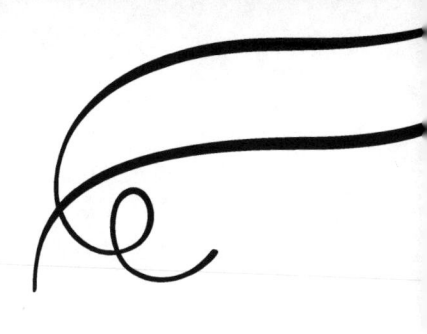

Age 12 and 13: Junior High

The First Day of Phys Ed

It was the first day of seventh grade. Junior high! Whoa, I was finally out of grade school. And feeling pretty mature, I have to tell you.

Everything was so different. I didn't have one teacher; I had six. There were a *lot* more kids, most of whom I'd never met. It was fun. But a little scary. All of a sudden, life seemed more real somehow.

So I was already a little overwhelmed when I walked in to phys ed second period.

It was the first day of school, so of course nobody had their gym clothes. Until Mr. Paskvan, our phys ed teacher, told us, we didn't know what kind of clothes were required. We sat in the gym while he told us what to expect this year, including what gym clothes were.

They were all pretty standard, pretty much what I'd expected. Shorts, T-shirt, sneakers. This was, of course, a boys-only class, so none of this was new to us. But then he told us we'd need to purchase an athletic supporter.

If you're not real familiar with the term, that's completely understandable for two reasons. First, almost nobody wears one anymore, and second, most people use the more familiar term: jock strap.

Yes, we had to buy a jock strap. That is not something us little kids had ever done. I didn't really know what one was, except that we wore it in place of underwear. But not a problem. They sold them at Lake Erie Sports, the sporting goods store downtown.

Back in those days, our small town had most kinds of stores. The things we'd buy today at Walmart or Home Depot, we would buy in small stores downtown. So of course we had a sporting goods store.

That day after school, I rode my bike downtown and walked into Lake Erie Sports to buy an athletic supporter.

I was a little nervous. No, that's a lie. I was extremely nervous. I'm guessing it's similar to the first time a girl has to buy a bra, or something like that. I didn't know where in the store they would be, and I wasn't even 100 percent sure what they looked like.

When I walked in, the nice lady who worked there, Mrs. Martin, said, "Can I help you?"

Why did it have to be a woman? Couldn't it have been a man? Did I really have to talk to this middle-aged woman about clothing that is supposed to protect…that? Really?

But I had no choice. In my high-pitched prepubescent voice, as calmly and as manly as I could, I said, "I need an athletic supporter."

She smiled at me (of course she did) and took me to a counter against the wall that had a bunch of small brown paper bags stapled shut. Again, really? Not boxes? Something with a picture on it? Maybe directions about how to wear it? Give me some info about the thing? But no, they really were in brown paper bags.

To me, they all looked the same. Then she asked the dreaded question: "What size?"

What size? What size? Well, I was eleven years old; puberty was many years away. I was about 4'11" and ninety pounds. Obviously, I was very small. But she could see that, so I figured that wasn't what she was asking. By "What size?," I assumed she meant, "What size is your…?"

Again, really? I froze. Was I really supposed to tell this woman some intimate details about me? What size?

I was a tiny kid. But I wasn't about to say "small." No guy would *ever* say that. I knew she wouldn't believe me if I said "large." So I gave the only answer I could: "Medium."

She picked up one of the brown paper bags and asked, "Will that be all?"

Hell yes, that was all. Please give it to me and I'll run right out the door. How embarrassing. I paid for the jock strap, flew out the door, got on my bike and rode home. Phew!

It wasn't until later that I realized she was asking my waist size, not the size of…something else. But I didn't know that then. Looking back, even though Mrs. Martin was a nice lady, I'm not 100 percent convinced she didn't get some kind of perverse pleasure by making little kids like me squirm.

THE FIRST DAY OF PHYS ED

I survived that trauma. Really, Dad should have come with me to do it, but as always, he was working. So my eleven-year-old self faced the trauma, and lived another day.

But really, Mrs. Martin could have made the experience a lot easier.

I Learned a Lesson

One Saturday afternoon, my dad and I went to visit his parents, Grandpa Whitey and Grandma Mercedes (pronounced mer-SEED-us). Great Aunt Mabel was also there. While we visited Mom's mom and dad all the time, we didn't visit Dad's side too often. Dad didn't know his dad or stepmom that well, having been raised by his grandparents after his mom died. So I didn't really know them all that well either.

For whatever reason, this visit was a little unusual. Especially since it was just me and Dad. I don't remember the purpose of the visit, or why Aunt Mabel was there. Like old people do, they sat around and talked. And talked. I was bored. I mean, I was just a kid, and nothing they had to say interested me. In the least.

Being the good kid I always tried to be, I sat and listened. I don't remember complaining or whining. However, when I did join in the conversation…it went something like this.

Aunt Mabel asked, "How's school going?" That's what old people always ask kids when they try to talk to them. Because they don't know what else to ask. In fact, I find myself asking the exact same question when I'm talking to a student I don't know very well. I'm just like Aunt Mabel in that respect, I guess.

I LEARNED A LESSON

I have no idea how this came up, but we must have been talking about math, because Aunt Mabel said to me, "Yeah, they don't learn you good arithmetic these days."

I thought, *Learn you? Really, Aunt Mabel? Don't you mean teach you?* Now, I know Aunt Mabel was raised in the days when not everyone went to high school, or even past sixth grade. I also know sometimes people don't have perfect grammar. Still, to be honest, I was a bit annoyed she was criticizing my education while using really bad, no-good, horrible grammar. What's more, she was wrong. They *did* teach us math. A lot of it. And I was pretty good at it.

Of course, what I should have done was…nothing. Or just smiled. Or at the most, maybe said something like, "Oh no, we spend a lot of time on math, and I'm pretty good at it."

I didn't do any of those things. Instead, I had one of those moments when my mouth spoke before my brain could intervene. We all have those moments. (Some of us more than others!) Before I could stop myself, I said, "Yeah, and they didn't learn you very good English back in the day."

Okay, that was *not* the respectful answer I should have given. And I immediately knew it. But it was out, and I couldn't un-say it.

Not much happened. Nobody yelled at me; nobody seemed offended. (We're often very good at hiding that kind of emotion.) Shortly thereafter, Dad and I said our goodbyes and left to drive home.

Somehow, I knew that wouldn't be the end of it. And it wasn't. The moment our car left the driveway, Dad exploded.

Now, my dad wasn't big on life lessons, if for no other reason than he wasn't home very much. But this time was different. For the next few minutes, I was lectured about respect for elders, keeping my mouth shut, learning appreciation for relatives, and on and on.

I couldn't argue. He was right. I had been disrespectful, and I knew it. No, Mabel wasn't the most educated person, but that didn't mean she was stupid, and I didn't have to mock her for it. But sometimes kids are not as nice as they should be. This was one of those times.

It became a learning moment. I won't be so stupid to say I never disrespected anyone after that. However, I was more careful. And I'm pretty sure I treated my elders just a bit better from then on.

So Dad, in this case anyway, did manage to teach a life lesson. One I heard and understood.

While I shouldn't have said it, the lasting result was a little bit of awareness. And that's a good thing.

The Worst Christmas Program

I was twelve, and my church was getting ready for its annual Christmas program. They were pretty much the same every year, and probably at almost every church. We'd all dress up in really bad costumes and act out the nativity. Most kids had a few lines to say, but some parts were a little easier. For instance, while the shepherds and wise men had a lot to say, those of us who were sheep, cattle, or donkeys didn't have to say a word.

One year, I was a shepherd, complete with a bad imitation of a shepherd's crook, a really bad robe, and an impossibly unrealistic fake beard. I had about two lines, which I practiced forever, and I spoke them without a mistake. Whew!

But when I was twelve, I was considered one of the big kids. The program director let me pick my part. I could choose Joseph or a wise man. Joseph, of course, was a starring role, on stage through the entire pageant, but didn't have a speaking part. I guess Joseph was a man of few words, maybe. A wise man was a much smaller part, but had about four lines to recite.

I thought about this for a long time. On one hand, the wise man part sounded more fun. But on the other hand...

Well, here was the problem: I had a huge crush on Kathy Jensen, the girl chosen to play Mary. If I chose to be Joseph, I'd be around her for all the practices and the program itself.

I'm not sure why this seemed so important, because I went to school and Sunday school with this girl, and I saw her often. Still, I couldn't get past that I'd get to be by her for all that time.

The other trouble was that whichever part I didn't choose, Tommy would get. Tommy was a nice kid, but we didn't know each other that well. We hung out with different groups. And Tommy had significant learning difficulties. I thought about the four lines he'd have to memorize and recite. I knew he'd have trouble. And I knew the right thing to do would be to choose the wise man, so he could be Joseph and be spared having to memorize those lines.

Honestly, I agonized about this. In the end, selfishness won. I chose to be Joseph. Tommy would be the wise man. He didn't complain. I think he was fine with it. I felt a little better.

We had three or four practices, and each time, Tommy struggled with his lines. He just couldn't get the words out. He didn't seem to remember them. I told myself it was too late to switch, and that it might seem too obvious if I suggested it. So I didn't say a word.

The big night came. We got all dressed up and went to our places. When the cue came, Mary and Joseph walked out and huddled near the manger, where we'd stay for the duration. The sheep and cows did their parts just fine, as did the shepherds, and almost everyone. But when the wise men came on stage, I got worried.

The first two wise men were fine, but when it was Tommy's turn, he struggled just like he had in practice. He just stood there, with everyone looking at him. The director tried to whisper his lines, and that helped, a little. But it was obvious he couldn't do it. If he had been a little kid, nobody would have thought anything of it. But he was thirteen I think, and everyone could see what was happening. The church was filled with mostly good people, so of course nobody laughed at him. But Tommy knew, and while he didn't say anything, I know he was embarrassed.

Almost sixty years later, I still think about that. I know I was only twelve, but I shouldn't have been so selfish. On the one hand, I give myself some credit for thinking about giving him the easy part. But in the end, thinking about it wasn't enough, and my selfishness caused Tommy some embarrassment and a bit of humiliation. Really, I screwed up.

I still hear from Tommy occasionally on social media. He's doing okay. That one night didn't ruin him, of course. But still, I could have saved him from that humiliation, and I didn't.

If any good came from it, it was that I didn't forget that. I knew I'd try harder in the future to save people from that kind of embarrassment. While I don't know if I've succeeded, I do know that I do often try.

So who knows; maybe Tommy's troubles taught me enough to save others from that same fate for the next half century. I don't know. I just hope so. Because I can still remember Tommy's face when he was struggling.

And I still blame myself.

Girls

Dick Morgan – Mary Jane
Jeff Morgan

The tea party

  Our neighborhood had lots of boys about the same age. But we only had one girl, Mary Jane, Davey's little sister. As I've said, we didn't play with her much. I'm not sure why, because she was kinda a tomboy. But still, mostly our play was just the boys. Mary Jane didn't hang out with us.

Not that we wouldn't have allowed her to. I just don't think she found the stuff we did much fun. Mary Jane was cute, with long brown hair. In fact, when I was very young, I kinda thought long hair was the only real difference between boys and girls. I mean, I was the youngest, and I had never seen my sisters without their clothes on. I didn't realize at such a young age about those differences. But not only was Mary Jane cute, she was nice, too. While I do remember she and I having a tea party in the garage, we didn't play together that much. So while she may be the first not-related girl I knew, she wasn't a "girlfriend."

When I got to the grand old age of five, I was in the first grade. There were *lots* of girls in first grade. But I was still pretty much oblivious to the whole "girlfriend" thing. That was, until Lynn kissed me. Yes, she actually kissed me. I was only in first grade, and the only girls I had ever kissed were in my family. I just couldn't figure out what Lynn was doing, or why she was doing it. All I know is, she ran up to me, kissed me on the cheek, then ran away. What did I do? I cried. I was so upset. It must have been right after school, because I went home and told Mom about it, still crying. I'm pretty sure Mom had a difficult time holding in her laughter. But it was so traumatic. And to make it worse, later in first grade, Peggy kissed me. Two in one year! I don't think I cried that time, though it still bothered me.

But still, there was no girl I could call a girlfriend.

Until fifth grade. That year, Sue was new to our school. And I thought she was beautiful. Now, when you're in fifth grade, you're not supposed to like girls. Or you can't admit it if you do. (At least that was the case in 1965.) I couldn't actually tell anybody I liked her. I had to keep it to myself. But the cool thing was that Sue and I were two of the top students in the class. We always had a friendly competition about our grades. It gave me an excuse to talk to her and hang out. I think I was starting to realize that girls were somehow different.

Sadly, Sue was *not* in my sixth-grade class. I was so upset, although I couldn't show it of course. I found out later that my fifth-grade teacher, Mr. Davis, specifically did this. He told my mom he didn't think I should be competing with a girl! To this day, that doesn't make sense to me. In sixth grade, if someone is not in your class, you never see them. So Sue kinda just faded away, and by seventh grade she had moved away, never to be heard from again.

But then, in eighth grade, I met Sue Ann. Now, eighth graders are an odd lot. Some of the boys had already hit puberty, and were tall, strong, and hairy! But that wasn't me. I was years away from that growth spurt. While those more "mature" boys might have thought about girls like adults do, that wasn't me. I just knew I liked Sue Ann. I liked being around her, talking to her. But again, I couldn't tell anyone, *especially* not Sue Ann.

That summer, I happened to ride my bike by her house. Quite often. It was a little tricky, because she lived on a dead-end street. So it was hard to be nonchalant about it. Still, she quite often just happened to be outside. Which was really cool. That summer, we hung out quite a bit. But I was still mostly a little kid. So all we did was ride our bikes, and talk. That was it. I didn't know what more there was.

It was a little difficult; since I couldn't admit I liked a girl, I couldn't call her up or anything like that. Instead, I had to rely on us just kinda running into each other. Which happened quite often. So that summer was my "Sue Ann summer."

Now, I'm sure my family figured it out, even though I couldn't tell them. I couldn't even talk about Sue Ann. That would be giving it away. But one day, I almost blew it. I'd been riding my bike downtown, and in front of the library, I came across Sue Ann riding her bike. (That was pretty much how all of our meetings started—by intentional accident.) But that evening at supper, I forgot I had to keep all this a secret, and I said, "I was riding by the library today." And then I just stopped. Right there, in mid-sentence. I was about to say I had seen Sue Ann. But I couldn't, because that would be giving it all away.

I remember my whole family looking at me, waiting for the rest. But I never finished the sentence. I just kept eating, pretending it hadn't happened. Luckily, they didn't push me. I'm pretty sure they all knew, and were nice enough to let me pretend I didn't have a girlfriend.

By the next year, it had run its course. We still saw each other at school, but it wasn't the same. I'm not sure why. Of course, we couldn't talk about it, because we had to pretend we didn't like each other. So we just kinda drifted. And later that year she moved away. Honestly, I'm still kinda sad about that. I'm not 100 percent sure I treated her fairly.

Another girlfriend gone. As I grew up, of course, I had real girlfriends, eventually got married, had kids, the whole nine yards. But I still remember Lynn and that first kiss.

And that I cried.

Roller Skating

Near Port Clinton is a place called Catawba Island, which isn't really an island. It's an area farther out on our peninsula, just a few miles away. And on Catawba Island is Gem Beach. Today, it's a pretty upscale community, with nice homes, marinas, boat storage, and the like. But years ago, it had a lot more.

It had a dance hall my sisters would go to. Actually, I think my mom and dad met there, so it had been around quite a while. I was not cool enough to go dancing. But Gem Beach also had a roller rink, and I definitely went there a lot.

I think I started going in seventh grade. But of course, we didn't drive, and Gem Beach is too far to ride our bikes. Mom or Dad could have driven us I suppose, but that meant they'd have to drop us off *and* pick us up. So that didn't happen. But there was another way.

Mr. Butler, just some guy who liked roller skating, used to drive us out there. Not us particularly, but anybody who wanted to go. I have no idea how all this came about, but Mr. Butler parked an old school bus in the junior high parking lot. And every Friday night during the summer, he took whoever showed up out to the skating rink. Me, Dick, and Andy, used to walk down there and pay our fare, which I think was twenty-five cents, and included the transportation *and* admission to the skating rink. (I think Jeff went too, but no way was he going to hang out with his little brother!) Mr. Butler would drive us out there, make sure we all went to the roller rink and *not* the dance hall, then go in and skate. When the night was done, he'd drive us all back to the junior high. Then we'd walk home.

Keep in mind that there was no FBI background check, no vetting, no nothing. I don't think my parents even really knew much about him. And also, he drove a school bus. He drove us all. With no permission slips, no waivers, no nothing. I don't think that happens today.

Skating was a lot of fun, for the most part. I mean, all my friends were there. There were snacks and drinks, and even pinball games. So that was neat.

Most of the time was considered "all skate." Taped organ music would play, and we'd all skate in a counterclockwise circle. I was never a fancy skater. I couldn't go backward, for instance. Mostly, I think I just skated and talked to my friends.

But there were a couple "specials." There was "ladies only" when all the girls would go out and skate, doing circles and spins (if they could) and things like that. Then there was "men only." When that came, all us guys did one thing: we skated as fast as we could. Showing off for the girls I guess, although that was kinda lost on me. I just skated fast because everyone else did.

Then there was "couples only." I liked that because there was absolutely no way I was going to ask a girl to skate with me, so that was the time I'd play pinball.

But the worst one was "ladies' choice." Ugh. I did *not* want to skate with a girl. But if asked, I knew it would be rude to say no. It wasn't just about skating with a girl; all the couples were holding hands! And dancing on their skates. And stuff like that. I wanted no part of that. So to make sure I wasn't asked, when I heard the PA announcer say, "Ladies' choice," I'd head right to the men's room. They couldn't ask me if they couldn't find me. Worked every time!

Gem Beach, like many things in our area, was only a summer thing. There was no skating in the winter. So two churches in town, the Methodist and the Lutheran, opened their fellowship halls for roller skaters. I've been in both of those places recently, and they really aren't very big. But we made it work. We skated there lots of times in the winter.

By about the end of junior high, we stopped going. Whether we outgrew it, or the place closed, or Mr. Butler didn't drive anymore, I have no idea.

Gem Beach skating was great, but like so many things in our lives, it ran its course. I'm not sure I've ever roller skated again.

But boy, those Friday nights were fun. Even if I had to hide from the girls!

A Trip to Remember

Drinking "wine" at Put-In-Bay

    I didn't make much money on my paper route. But I made *some*, and I decided to use it for something special.

    How special? Well, my friend Dick and I wanted to take a trip. All by ourselves. Of course, we were only twelve, so that wouldn't seem possible. Yet...Dick and I decided to save up for a trip to Put-in-Bay. For those who don't know, Put-in-Bay is a tiny town on South Bass Island, about twelve miles north in Lake Erie. For those who do know, yes, it's sometimes considered a "Sodom and Gomorrah" type place. If you've ever been there on a weekend, you definitely would *not* let a kid go there by himself. These days, it's wildly popular in the summer months. And rowdy. And loud. And...not kid-friendly. (Although, years later, as a cross country coach, I periodically had cross country camp at Put-in-Bay. We always went during the week, and it was fine, completely safe, and a lot of fun.)

Back to 1968. Things were different then, and going to Put-in-Bay was our plan. Honestly, I don't remember if we even asked our parents. Maybe we did. Somehow, we assumed we'd be allowed. At the age of twelve!

For months, we talked about it. Andy was supposed to go with us as well. Honestly, he was the only one of the three of us who made real money from the paper route. But Andy backed out of the trip. I think he wanted to save up his money for a drum set. We were disappointed, but we decided to go anyway, just the two of us.

We saved, we planned, and we figured out everything we were going to do and how we were going to get there. Remember, it's an island; we couldn't just have Mom drive us there. But hey, we didn't let obstacles like that get in our way. We were going to go!

So one day that summer, we made it happen.

The only way to Put-in-Bay is by boat or by plane. We decided to do both! We rode our bikes to the ferry dock downtown and picked up a schedule. A paper schedule, kinda like a brochure. Remember them? No webpage, email, Facebook page, or anything like that back in the 60s. If you wanted a schedule, you had to pick one up. We rode our bikes to the airport to get their schedule as well. Yes, Port Clinton had (and still has) an airport. Back then, they had regularly scheduled flights to Put-in-Bay. They advertised it as "The Shortest Scheduled Airline in the World." I think they were correct.

When the big day came, we stashed our bikes in Mom's trunk and she drove us to the ferry dock. We dropped our bikes off and paid the fares, then Mom took us to the airport.

We went in and bought our tickets (I think they were $1.75, but I could be wrong). And we boarded the Tin Goose. I know there are a few of these planes left; now they're mostly novelties. The official name is Ford Tri-Motor because they have three propellors. Periodically I still see them flying around Port Clinton, but they're just for show. Kinda like antique planes or something. But in 1968, they were in regular use for this airline. I remember getting on the plane, and it was not exactly luxury. I mean really no big deal, since the flight only lasted about fifteen minutes, maybe less. There weren't even real seats. We sat on some metal slats mounted just above the floor. But hey, we were flying.

Now I had never been on a plane before, and I was petrified. But I sucked it up and got on. Good thing Put-in-Bay wasn't far, because Dick and I both have memories of looking down, and we were pretty sure the cars were going faster than us. Probably not true, but it sure seemed like it. (The truth is not far off. That plane cruises anywhere between 60 and 120 MPH. When I see them in the skies today, they look like they're hardly moving at all.)

After a few minutes over land, the plane headed out over Lake Erie, and landed on the island. Success, right? Well, kinda sorta—because the airport is almost two miles from the ferry dock in downtown PIB. I don't think we had thought that through. But hey, no problem. We just walked all the way into town, went to the dock, and picked up our bikes.

We spent the entire day there. Since it was over fifty years ago, I can't remember all the details. I remember riding our bikes all over the place. We went to the winery and bought some sparkling grape juice and pretended we were drinking wine. I think we did some miniature golf, and we probably went to the cave. I *know* we went up in Perry's Monument, a 352-foot-tall tower officially called the "Perry's Victory and International Peace Memorial," built to commemorate General Oliver Hazard Perry's victory over the British in the War of 1812. It reminds me of the Washington Memorial. If you ever go to Put-in-Bay, you really have to go up in the monument. It's a pretty cool view.

We had a great time, but a day doesn't last forever. When it was time to go home, we went to the ferry dock, paid for our bikes and ourselves, and took the ferry home. The ferry in those days went pretty slowly; I think it took about an hour and a half to get home. Once there, we got on our bikes and rode home. A successful and memorable short vacation.

But let's think through that. We were twelve years old. Twelve! How many parents would let their twelve-year-old son go on a vacation like that without an adult today? Nope, nobody would. If they did, they'd probably get arrested for child endangerment! But those were different times. We never thought it might be dangerous. Apparently our parents didn't either. At the time, it only seemed fun. It didn't seem to be a big deal. It was just something we did.

I'm glad we went. I'm glad Mom and Dad were, somehow, okay with it. I'm glad we could save the money to go. And I'm glad I got that experience. I mean, decades later, I still remember it. My first time on a ferry, my first time on a plane, my first time on a trip without my parents. What a day. It's too bad kids today can't do something like that.

It made an amazing memory.

Afterword

As you've read, I seem to remember a lot of details from the past. Consequently, I tell a lot of stories—some from recent times, some from my childhood. One day my wife said, "Why don't you write these down?" So I started to write stories from my childhood. I didn't really think they had any value. And I didn't think anyone outside of my immediate family would care to read them. But I started writing anyway.

When I was a good way into the project, I saw a social media video of a flash mob in Germany. It started with a little girl on a recorder and a man on an upright bass playing Beethoven's "Ode to Joy." Gradually other musicians joined in. A crowd gathered, the musicians played, and within six minutes it was a full-fledged concert, people loving every minute of it.

When I saw that, I immediately thought three things.

One: I would *love* to have written anything close to as good as "Ode to Joy." But hey, I'm not Beethoven, so I can't feel too bad about that.

Two: I would *love* to be a performer in a flash mob. I play the piano, so maybe that could work. It would be so much fun.

Three: During the flash mob, the video of course showed all the people watching. And there was a short, maybe two-second clip of a very old man being helped along by a younger woman, probably his daughter. Somehow, I connected with that old man in the two seconds he was shown. While he was old, and maybe not making a difference to the world anymore, at one time he'd had a full life. He'd had a family, a job, experiences. He had lived! All of which was important to him, and his loved ones. I realized that when that old man dies, all those experiences and memories will be…gone. Nobody will know them, remember them, or value them. And it made me very sad.

In that moment, I vowed to finish these stories and get them published. Now, in the scheme of the world, I'm pretty much a nobody. I'm not famous, so maybe nobody will care about my childhood. But I've realized it doesn't matter. Because if I tell these stories, they won't die with me. They'll continue on. Even if the only people to read the book will be my relatives and close friends, that's okay. While I'd love it if other people read it, that's not the most important thing. By putting these down on paper, they won't die with me. They'll be my own odd sort of immortality, I guess. The stories will be here, maybe as just words on a page, but they'll be here. And if anyone ever wants to read them, they can.

That's why this book is here.

These are the stories that made me who I am. As Miranda Lambert sings, they're the stories "that built me." Some are good, some are silly, some are sad, some are happy, some are thoughtful. They're all part of my memories, my experiences, my life.

AFTERWORD

I'm not that much younger than the man in the flash mob video. So, I knew I better get going. While yesterday definitely happened, tomorrow is never promised.

I hope at least some of these stories have struck a chord with you. I hope they brought back some of your memories. I hope they brought you some moments of thoughtfulness. But most of all, I hope they made you smile.

Writing them brought joy to me. I hope they did the same for you.